Strategic Intelligence and Civil Affairs to Understand Legitimacy and Insurgency

Diane E. Chido

Strategic Intelligence and Civil Affairs to Understand Legitimacy and Insurgency

Avoiding the Stabilization Trap

palgrave
macmillan

Diane E. Chido
DC Analytics
Erie, PA, USA

ISBN 978-3-030-20976-6   ISBN 978-3-030-20977-3   (eBook)
https://doi.org/10.1007/978-3-030-20977-3

This Palgrave Pivot imprint is published by the registered company Springer Nature
Switzerland AG
The registered company address is: Gewerbestrasse 11, 6330 Cham, Switzerland

This book is dedicated to the two most important men in my life, my beloved son, Zachary, and my beloved partner, Matthew. Thank you both for your endless love and support.

FOREWORD

I remember when I first arrived in Skopje, Macedonia, in 1994. Just a few blocks from the office building that housed the US mission (there was no embassy, yet) was a shopping district. Macedonia was the poorest of the former Yugoslav Republics and was embargoed from the south by Greece and asked to enforce sanctions to the north against Serbia.

Despite all this, in the middle of this shopping district, there were perhaps a dozen kiosks all selling gold. Each did a brisk business. Every day, dozens of people showed up, made their purchases, and left. Indeed, of all the shops in the market, these were among the busiest.

This surprised me. Amidst all the poverty, in the middle of a war, with factories shuttered, and enemies to both the north and south, who had the money or the interest to buy gold?

As I watched more closely, it became clear what was happening. Customers would bring wads of newly minted Macedonian Denars, well-travelled Deutsche Marks, or even US Dollars and exchange them for just a few links of gold. They weren't buying jewelry, they were preparing for when this latest experiment in governance failed.

Most of the Macedonians alive at that time had lived in three countries without ever changing address. The only economy that worked was the informal one. The only thing that was certain was that someone else was calling the shots—but that they were in the line of fire.

How does someone survive, take care of their children, their family, in such a situation? In a word—relationships. In these kinds of environments, you are either part of "us" or part of "them." If you are "us," then helping you makes us stronger, more resilient. If you are part of "them," however, you are just a tool to be used or an enemy to be thwarted by any means possible.

Stability is much less common than those in the developed world would like to admit. In unstable environments, where relationships matter most, what gets done is less important to the local players than who does it. Breaking promises to support me and mine is not only allowed, it is expected.

Failure to understand and appreciate the role of relationships in stability operations has very real costs. In other countries in similar situations, I have seen shops full of reasonably priced goods despite government promises to enforce sanctions or embargoes. I have had local bankers, once I got to know them, tell me that they quite literally made up all the numbers they briefed so convincingly the day before to international investors. I have even had our putative allies sign contracts with their putative enemy, while they were talking to me (unaware that I read and spoke the local language).

Diane Chido knows all of this. She has spent decades working, understanding, travelling, and living in foreign countries. More importantly, she has spent almost as much time studying the cultures, tribes, languages, economies, leaders, and people that make up much of the unstable part of the world. Her observations are informed by both experience and research and are the better for it.

Is this to say that this slim volume is the final word on the topic? No. But it is a useful addition to the debate. The dangers of an unstable world are too numerous and dire to ignore. As the pace of technology quickens and threats proliferate, there is no excuse for not challenging conventional wisdom and recasting our mental models of how the world really works. In these two things, this monograph succeeds admirably.

Department of Intelligence Studies   Kristan J. Wheaton
Mercyhurst University
Erie, PA, USA

PREFACE

The purpose of this study was to delve into the *Guiding Principles for Stabilization and Reconstruction*, particularly the entwined issues of Stable Governance and Social Well-Being as they appear not from the policy-maker perspective, but from that of the population upon whom policies are enacted. This monograph recommends that the US begin to identify opportunities for enhancing legitimacy by supporting some types of alternative governance it otherwise might view as threats to state authority, failing to recognize that hierarchical, centralized states are not the only effective governing structures. The Army should enhance and redirect its strategic intelligence and Civil Affairs capabilities toward these efforts.

Erie, PA

Diane E. Chido

ACKNOWLEDGMENTS

This research was generously funded and guided by the US Army Peace Keeping and Stability Operations Institute (PKSOI), without which it would not exist. Special thanks go to all my friends and colleagues who took the time to share their expertise and provide comments and enthusiastic discussions as this work evolved. You have been too generous to be implicated in the final product, thus all errors are mine. Thanks to Colonels Brendan Arcuri, Jay Liddick, Steve Marr, Dan O'Rourke, Ms. Tamara Fitzgerald, Mr. Scott Braderman, and especially Mr. Ryan McCannell, who hated it, so his comments were a big help. Eternal gratitude to Mr. Jim Cooney, who, thanks to his shared interest and expertise in governance, helped me talk (and talk) through it all. Thanks to Ms. Anca Pusca and Ms. Katelyn Zingg for their support and production skills.

ABOUT THE BOOK

This book describes the common pitfalls of US military interventions in efforts at stabilization, which supports post-conflict societies by establishing stable governance, rule of law, a safe and secure environment, economic development, and social well-being for all members of the population. These efforts are often unsuccessful and can even cause harm when mission teams do not understand the populations with whom they are interacting and when policymakers, who also lack this knowledge, fail to plan appropriate strategy and missions. The book recommends prioritizing a relational approach to stabilization with a professional and well-resourced Civil Affairs and strategic intelligence approach to engagements over the current preference for transactional, often lethal operations.

CONTENTS

About the Author

Diane E. Chido is founder of Erie, PA-based research firm, DC Analytics, and a former faculty instructor and project advisor for the Mercyhurst University Department of Intelligence Studies. Diane recently completed a three-year contract serving as the Security and Intelligence Policy Advisor to the US Army's Peace Keeping and Stability Operations Institute (PKSOI) housed at the US Army War College in Carlisle, PA. Diane has over 25 years of experience supporting post-conflict and fragile societies, beginning as a research assistant with the Brookings Institution's Foreign Policy Program working on Russia's early transition to democracy and on African development. At the International Monetary Fund in the mid-1990s, she participated in numerous economic reporting missions to Belarus, Russia, and Ukraine. She has published and lectured widely on topics related to alternative governance, intelligence, legitimacy, security, sociocultural issues, stabilization, security sector assistance and reform, telecommunications, and the challenges of the dense urban environment.

ABBREVIATIONS

COO	Center for Complex Operations
CPS	Criminalized Power Structures
DDR	Disarmament, Demobilization, and Reintegration
DNI	Director of National Intelligence
DoD	US Department of Defense
DoDD	Department of Defense Directive
DoS	US Department of State
EU	European Union
IMU	Islamic Movement of Uzbekistan
JCIC	Joint Concept for Integrated Campaigning
JP 3-24	Joint Operations Doctrine on Counterinsurgency
MNLA	Movement for the National Liberation of Azawad
MOE	Measure of Effectiveness
MOP	Measure of Performance
NATO	North Atlantic Treaty Organization
NDS	National Defense Strategy
ODNI	Office of the Director of National Intelligence
PKSOI	Peace Keeping and Stability Operations Institute
SAR	Stabilization Assistance Review
TRADOC	Training and Doctrine Command
UN	United Nations
UNMINUSMA	United Nations Multidimensional Integrated Stabilization Mission in Mali
USAFRICOM	US Africa Command
USAID	US Agency for International Development
USG	US Government

LIST OF FIGURES

INTRODUCTION

Abstract When the US commits to stability operations, it must focus on long-term legitimacy to prevent falling into the *Stability Trap*. Despite substantial doctrine, policy, and historical examples attesting to the complexities of stabilization, the US Army tends to have an oversimplified view of stability as a *transactional* series of short-term tasks; conversely, for the state it is supporting, stabilization is a long-term *relational* process of rebuilding its legitimacy with the people and reestablishing governance. Rarely are US policymakers, including military leaders, willing or able to plan for the long-term development of these relationships between post-conflict states and their societies. This monograph recommends that the US Army begin to identify opportunities for enhancing legitimacy by supporting some types of alternative governance it otherwise might view as threats to state authority, failing to recognize that hierarchical, centralized states are not the only effective governing structures.

Keywords Stability • Legitimacy • Governance • Alternative governance • Strategic intelligence • Civil Affairs

When the US commits to stability operations, it must focus on long-term legitimacy to prevent falling into the *Stability Trap*. This challenge is similar to the *Liberator's Dilemma* described by LTC Joseph Long, Chief of Special Forces Proponency, in which "responsibility for a population inherently transfers from the original governing body to the liberating military forces." In his treatise on guerrilla leadership, LTC Long further noted, "Negative framing can result in unanticipated audience costs that reduce trust and increase tension between forces reliant on long-term American support and create a reputation where the U.S. continues to make false promises."[1] Therefore, foreknowledge and situational understanding are likely to go a long way to reduce this tendency toward false promises, thus increasing the Stabilizer's legitimacy before and after action and thus its likelihood of establishing long-term stability.

Despite substantial doctrine, policy, and historical examples attesting to the complexities of stabilization, the US Army tends to have an oversimplified view of stability as a *transactional* series of short-term tasks; conversely, for the state it is supporting, stabilization is a long-term *relational* process of rebuilding its legitimacy with the people and reestablishing governance. Rarely are US policymakers, including military leaders, willing or able to plan for the long-term development of these relationships between post-conflict states and their societies.

This monograph recommends that the US Army begin to identify opportunities for enhancing legitimacy by supporting some types of alternative governance it otherwise might view as threats to state authority, failing to recognize that hierarchical, centralized states are not the only effective governing structures. Understanding the sources of legitimacy, vulnerabilities within a state will also enable *Stabilizers* to identify what sort of alternative governance structures are likely to arise when the state does not have the trust of the population and how and whether to counter, coopt, or cooperate with them. Within the construct of "the state," this monograph views any political entity from a municipal, to a provincial, to a federal unit claiming sovereign authority over a defined population in a structure granted legitimacy by the Western model of democracy.[2]

Outsiders are likely to have difficulty understanding the complex social networks, incentives, and motivations that underlie these alternative forms of legitimacy, making it nearly impossible to determine with whom to negotiate to further US goals. In 1998, sociologist James C. Scott dubbed this Western inability to understand "illegibility"[3]; an apt term for this lack of capacity to "read" unfamiliar populations. US operatives must be able to gauge the amount and forms of power that members or leaders of such structures wield in actuality, as opposed to assurances they may give—especially in a climate of shifting alliances. This is where the role of an effective Civil Affairs (CA) capability is crucial. Throughout the long, turbulent American history of stabilization, which specifically requires the skills that only CA can bring to consolidating gains made through combat, CA has struggled to find its niche and ideal structure. This problem continues today.

Defense policy's framing of threats has coopted today's military intelligence capability to only look for operational threats and to identify, profile, and find artificially inflated "high-value targets" even in noncombat operational theaters. The resulting deaths of countless people since 2001 in at least 130 countries[4] have not enhanced understanding of sources of legitimacy and local grievances but have likely increased the latter.

In her 2011 report advocating for a school of military government, Rebecca Patterson of the Council on Foreign Relations (CFR) emphasized the traditional roles of strategic intelligence that have largely been lost in the current military intelligence environment, which now focuses on targeting. She recommended reviving, "An additional intelligence capability—one that provides early warning of civil unrest, study of politics and economics of specific areas of probable military concern, and analysis of key indicators that may illustrate a propensity for conflict."[5] This study supports that view and proposes developing an analytic toolkit for beginning to develop this shared capability within and between a better resourced Civil Affairs and resurrected Strategic Intelligence Analysis components.

NOTES

1. Joseph Long, "Framing Indigenous Leadership," *Advances in Social Sciences Research Journal.* March 2017, p. 250. Available from https://doi.org/10.14738/assrj.46.2936 accessed on May 22, 2018.
2. For more on the definition of a state and the concept of "softened sovereignty," see Anne L. Clunan and Harold A Trikunas, "Conceptualizing Ungoverned Spaces: Territorial Statehood, Contested Authority, and Softened Sovereignty," in Clunan and Trikunas eds., *Ungoverned Spaces: Alternatives to State Authority in an Era of Softened Sovereignty*, Stanford, CA: Stanford University Press, 2010, pp. 17–33.
3. James C. Scott, *Art of Not Being Governed: An Anarchist History of Upland Southeast Asia*, New Haven, CT: Yale University Press, 2010.
4. Andrew Cockburn, *Kill Chain: The Rise of the High-Tech Assassins*, New York, NY: Picador, 2015, p. 251. This number of 130 countries is a conservative estimate as Cockburn asserts that by 2015 such assassinations were taking place in over 120 countries and then relates how drone bases

have expanded since 2014. The estimate for this study only adds 10 to Cockburn's 120, but many other sources state the number is closer to 160.

5. Rebecca Patterson, "Revisiting a School of Military Government: How Reanimating a World War II-Era Institution Could Professionalize Military Nation Building," Ewing Marion Kauffman Foundation, June 2011, p. 18. Available from https://papers.ssrn.com/sol3/papers.cfm?abstract_id=1879444 accessed on May 7, 2018.

CHAPTER 1

Legitimacy and Governance in Stabilization

Abstract Understanding the sources of legitimacy within a state will enable those engaging in stabilization activities (*Stabilizers*) to identify what sort of alternative governance structures are likely to arise when the state does not have the trust of the population and how and whether to counter, coopt, or cooperate with them. Foreknowledge and situational understanding are likely to go a long way to reduce this tendency toward false promises, thus increasing the Stabilizer's and the sovereign's legitimacy before and after action and thus its likelihood of establishing long-term stability.

Keywords Stabilization • Governance • Alternative governance • Legitimacy • Competition • Insurgency

The US Government (USG) and international development organizations tend to treat *stable* governance as a key component of stability and a defense against complex challenges to universal democratic institution building. As illustrated in Fig. 1.1 from the *Guiding Principles of Stabilization and Reconstruction,* a publication generally considered the stabilization "bible," this *Strategic Framework* emphasizes stable governance as the "ability of the people to share, access, or compete for power through nonviolent political processes and to enjoy the collective benefits and services of the state."[1]

D. E. Chido, *Strategic Intelligence and Civil Affairs to Understand Legitimacy and Insurgency,*
https://doi.org/10.1007/978-3-030-20977-3_1

1

Fig. 1.1   Strategic framework for stabilization and reconstruction

This definition assumes two critical aspects of governance:

1. Competition for power must be nonviolent and conducted through established political processes
2. Services and other benefits are provided by the state to the assumed general satisfaction of the populace.

These highlighted aspects suggest a bias toward formal, state-based institutions at the expense of other, possibly competing forms of legitimacy, such as those arising in areas where the state's influence fails to reach. This state-based perspective limits the US and its partners to apply (overtly) its instruments of power in support of or in opposition to state structures only. This approach has positive and negative aspects, particularly in fragile or vulnerable states, whose populations are ambivalent about their government's ability or desire to provide basic public goods. In extreme cases, when the state has perpetrated violence against its own citizens, such as in the ongoing civil war in South Sudan, an approach focused on the state and its institutions is unlikely to result in lasting stability.

Those involved in the stabilization business, particularly when the US is the lead Stabilizer, often conflate *stable* governance with *good* governance and assume that stable governance, despite its form or quality, is preferable to instability. A United Nations University article from 2012 attempting to define this nebulous term determined that *good governance* "lacks parsimony, differentiation, coherence and theoretical utility."[2] The *Guiding Principles* support stable governance, defining it as "the mechanism through which the basic human needs of the population are largely met, respect for minority rights is assured, conflicts are managed peacefully through inclusive political processes, and competition for power occurs nonviolently."[3] National security experts often use the obvious example of North Korea as a state that appears to be stable, but no one believes its form of governance to be *good*, by any internationally accepted measure.

On the one hand, the US has a robust toolkit intended to reinforce governance through a myriad of mechanisms ranging from diplomacy to military intervention to financial and technical support via numerous government and nongovernmental agencies around the world. On the other hand, its bias toward formal, state-based structures can cause it to miss opportunities to clearly identify and, thereby, effectively shore up vulnerabilities in governance from the *people's* perspective, through which governance most importantly manifests itself as good or bad. This perspective should be the international actor's focus when considering pressures affecting the *state.*

In the case of stabilization activities, when a host nation invites entities of the US government to shore up vulnerabilities to stable governance in pre- or post-conflict circumstances, establishing and maintaining government legitimacy is the primary objective under which all other activities fall.[4] With this almost total focus on the host nation and international actors' objectives, the *Guiding Principles* recommend that Stabilizers, "Modify or use informal systems in combination with formal mechanisms to ensure adherence to international human rights standards while maximizing access and public trust in the system."[5] This only validates alternative governance when it suits the sensibilities of international standards, not local concerns or perspectives.

The *Guiding Principles* section on "Stable Governance" does suggest that Stabilizers "engage local leaders, civil society groups, and the general population through consultative or co-administrative mechanisms to ensure legitimacy of transitional governing structures,"[6] but the next sentence suggests "creating a political advisory council comprising host nation leaders," implying all members should be recognized by the host nation. Essentially, governance that the host nation government has not approved, nor aligned with, is illegitimate according to these standards for reconstruction and stabilization, which fail to acknowledge that identifying and understanding alternative governance structures is essential to the long-term success of any stabilization process.

Legitimacy and Insurgency

Legitimacy is the glue that holds any society together, whether it is as large and complex as a country or international institution like the European Union (EU) or as small and simple as a local Rotary Club. Legitimacy is a neutral concept only having a positive connotation to those who believe they possess it. The key for any governing entity to achieve or maintain legitimacy is trust, which a governing authority of any kind establishes by providing essential services. Such entities can range from a faith-based group, to a criminal gang, to a terrorist network.

The 2018 *Stabilization Assistance Review* (SAR), developed jointly by the US Departments of Defense (DoD), State (DoS), and the US Agency for International Development (USAID) stated, "Stabilization is most likely to be successful where there is basic security on the ground."[7] The SAR further emphasized the need for security and overall stabilization assistance and coordination with local actors to establish and maintain trust. At the most basic level, security allows establishment of predictability, which may be the very essence of this nebulous concept of "stability." After decades of civil war in Afghanistan, many people initially supported the Taliban, appreciating the "pattern of predictability, order and consistency," it provided.[8] This was also the case at first with the Islamic State, where Mosul residents told German journalist Jurgen Todenhofer that under Iraq's Shiite government they suffered from the chaos and initially thought they were better off under the Islamic State. Todenhofer noted, "instead of anarchy they have now law and order."[9]

Predictability may look nothing like stable governance as typically described, but it is, perhaps, the most basic human security need. Beyond Maslow's hierarchy of human needs,[10] which places physiological needs at the bottom of the pyramid and safety at the next lowest level, human security is more about the collective psychological needs of a given population. As David Kilcullen has noted, "Predictability is the basis for secure

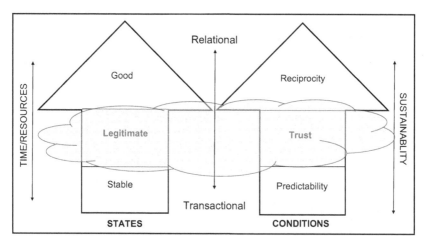

Fig. 1.2 Conceptualized governance hierarchy (Graphic produced by the author)

dispute resolution and thus for social stability."[11] Therefore, predictability may be a good start as an essential element of stability but remains within the realm of *transactional* legitimacy. As CNN journalist Fareed Zakaria opined while reporting on Todenhofer's research, "While there is an allure to security in the abstract, no one likes living under a brutal theocracy."[12]

The concept of "stable governance" requires the governing structure in question to provide a specific basket of goods and services as prioritized by the governed population, which tends to be highly dynamic. Figure 1.2 illustrates this elusive quality of legitimacy and its place in moving a society from stable to good governance, as it defines "good" for itself. Figure 1.2 also illustrates the need for a social structure to evolve from a *transactional* relationship between the governing and governed to a *relational* one or from basic predictability to reciprocity in which both support one another.

A legitimate relationship exists when a state and a people give and receive from each other *sustainable* predictability that enables economic growth and other conditions that allow a society to flourish at all levels. Sustainability in this arrangement depends upon the time and resources the governance entity is willing and able to expend on the society for each to perceive long-term mutual benefit. This is not simply composed of a constitution and grand buildings to house government institutions. The governance entity must build and maintain those institutions paying attention to the needs of the population it serves, not just serving up rhetoric about inclusivity and the rights of citizenship. A self-serving governance structure will ultimately foster the evolution of new forms of alternative governance without the development of a holistic society.

Although there may be some structures that are beneficial to the environment they operate in, the US tends to seek partners that speak English and feel familiar. Louise Wiuff Moe of the Finnish Institute for International Affairs noted, "The preference for ... rational-legal legitimacy, and the fact that the West finds such structures more readily understandable than many alternative authorities, may lead policymakers to choosing partners who excel at 'looking Western' rather than delivering results."[13] Such governance elements do not necessarily fake "Westerness," but American agents are likely to gravitate toward those that show affinity for their own preferences, which may not be the most culturally and ethnically effective measures in a stabilization environment.

Governance structures unwilling to collaborate with the US may actually be the most legitimate in some cases. That they want to operate independently and focus on their own constituents, rather than the international actors, may indicate an element of legitimacy that central governments in weak states are unable to attain. Dr. Todd Moss, now Senior Fellow at the Center for Global Development, stated in his 1995 anthology, "The argument that democracy should be encouraged in Africa as a means to securing political stability and economic prosperity is ungrounded and based on numerous false assumptions."[14] Then-Assistant Secretary of State for African Affairs, Herman Cohen, noted even earlier in a 1990 press release, "While the United States favors a multi-party system, who are we to say it is good for everybody?"[15] Even George Kennan acknowledged by 1989 that, "There are parts of the world where the main requirement of American security is not an unnatural imitation of the American model but sheer stability, and this last is not always assured by a government of what appears to be popular acclaim."[16]

Therefore, beyond predictability, the basket of goods that serve to ensure legitimacy is complex and dynamic, likely never to be the same for every population across space or time. Aleutian populations primarily require shelter and sufficiently warm clothing in order to conduct their daily lives in a remote and inhospitable climate replete with fresh water. With low population density and few dangerous neighbors or predators, individual members with harpoons, spears, firearms, and fire-starting capability can feel essentially secure without a national governance body providing security.

In contrast, desert nomads value access to water as the most precious need for their own and their livestock's security and will keep their neighbors feeling insecure to ensure their own supply. Nomads do not ask a central government to tell other nomad groups to stay away from their wells but manage these resources and their own security via a governance structure well understood by everyone in the neighborhood.

Most modern societies, on the other hand, inhabit increasingly urbanized environments that require governance structures to develop and maintain water and sanitation systems, electricity, and security in a space that packs many people together and must function as a complex society. Those on the fringe of that society, however, who live in neighborhoods lacking regular police patrols or reliable water, sanitation or electricity, or those squatting in makeshift homes or largely abandoned apartment buildings, must rely on alternative means for obtaining critical services. A criminal gang may provide predictable security and even daycare (Chicago, US)[17]; a single extended family may control the local water source and thus be a community leader (Mumbai, India)[18]; a group of entrepreneurs may obtain access to electrical power and users pay by the minute to charge their cell phones during a crisis (Port-au-Prince, Haiti).[19] The point is that, where there are people, there will be some kind of governance, but its legitimacy quotient may be fluid.

Legitimacy and Alternative Governance

All human groups, no matter their size or purpose, organize themselves into a power structure, as any social science text will attest. Someone always needs to be in charge of the various aspects of group activity and somebody, or many somebodies, must actually complete needed tasks, no matter how formally or informally this may be arranged. In fact, there likely are, and perhaps always have been, more alternative governance structures effectively providing stability than there are nation-states. Myriad descriptions can apply to the extent of the arrangement, but for this study, the construct will be the *Legitimacy Continuum*,[20] illustrated in Fig. 1.3.

Short-term groupings for immediate tasks, such as several neighbors pushing a car out of the snow on a winter day are *transactional*. No matter what kind of relationship some of the neighbors may have to each other— some may be close friends, others unknown to the rest, and some may have deep animosity toward each other—there is a job to be done and they

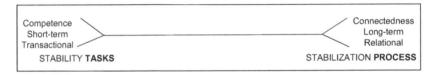

Competence Short-term Transactional	Connectedness Long-term Relational
STABILITY **TASKS**	STABILIZATION **PROCESS**

Fig. 1.3 The legitimacy continuum (Graphic produced by the author)

will work together to do it; the stability of the neighborhood depends upon it. This temporary grouping will exist only as long as needed to complete the task. Once the car is free and the driver on their way, the group disbands and moves on about their day, shoveling their own driveway or heading together to a popular sledding hill.

The legitimacy of this transactional arrangement is based purely on *competence*. If there is one driver (Person A) and three neighbors, one of the neighbors makes the decision to help (Person B). This automatically makes B the leader in the moral decision-making realm—the group recognizes B's competence for knowing when to do the "right thing," whether out of human kindness, to heal a rift among neighbors, or because B knows A will otherwise block *their* driveway if not assisted today.

Person C is the one who organizes the tasked group—this can also be B but could be a more practically minded neighbor who knows more about cars or who has lived longer in the Snow Belt. C organizes the group and instructs each on their task, maintaining legitimacy until the car is free or becomes more stuck—in the latter case, legitimacy may pass to another member of the team considered more competent to lead.

In other cases, transactional conditions can grow into connected relational conditions based on intangible alterations in the relationship that typically require time and a change in circumstances to take place. In the case of US security force assistance (SFA), the type and level of engagement occurs along a spectrum. In peacetime SFA, despite US doctrinal emphasis on relationship building,[21] the transactional relationship tends to dominate, as the assisted nation knows it can count on provision of US equipment and training but does not necessarily see the need for anything additional. In a combat environment, such as in Afghanistan or Iraq, competence in a transactional relationship may initially be sufficient. Over time, particularly if the threat remains relatively high, a relationship is likely to develop based upon common objectives (such as basic survival). This higher level of connectedness enables a longer term mutually beneficial engagement, leading to greater legitimacy of the combined operation. This assumes, of course, the Stabilizer exhibits at least a basic level of competence, thus giving the indigenous partner confidence in the Stabilizer's value.[22]

Transactional engagements have a measurable quality that make them appealing to the US government and the military in particular, as there is a tendency to prefer to count number of people trained, ammunition used, terrorists killed, territory held, or other highly tangible indicators that can easily be quantified because they are so concrete and "countable." However, such measures of *performance* (MOPs) do not truly measure mission or overall strategic objective attainment. More valuable are measures of *effectiveness* (MOEs), which should be more subjective with a longitudinal quality that exceeds simple "countablility." *US Military Doctrine Joint Publication on Stabilization (JP 3-07)* describes the difference between the two measures

> **MOPs** are indicators used to measure a friendly action that evaluates task accomplishment. The results of tactical tasks are often physical in nature, but also can reflect the impact on specific functions and systems. Use of MOPs in stabilization efforts should be tied to specific actions or tasks that support achievement of objectives.

> **MOEs** are indicators used to measure change in the attainment of an end state, achievement of an objective, or creation of an effect. MOEs can be based on quantitative or qualitative measures to reflect trends and show progress or regression toward a measurable threshold tied to specified desired effects or objectives of the stabilization efforts.[23]

MOEs' very nature make them more complex and difficult to formulate as metrics and more strenuous to determine qualitative results toward attainment. This challenge, coupled with the "mission accomplished" mindset that prefers to "go in—do the job—get out—go on to the next target," reduces the appeal of, and the capability for, effectively establishing and maintaining long-term relational, connected engagements.[24]

The problem is that legitimacy is a perception, and therefore difficult, but not impossible, to measure, particularly over time. Thus, one member of a group can believe they are part of a relational, long-term circumstance, while the other sees it as transactional and short-term, much like two humans after a one-night stand. This is often the case in stabilization operations when the short-term tasking creates a single-mission mindset without a clear understanding of the strategic objectives to which they contribute. Determining the level of legitimacy a supported host nation or stabilizing occupation has attained at defined time intervals is a worthwhile MOE to develop with the assistance of social scientists skilled in such assessments.

The US military's *Joint Operations Doctrine on Counterinsurgency (JP 3-24)* defines insurgency as "The organized use of subversion and violence to seize, nullify, or challenge political control of a region" noting the term can "also refer to the group itself."[25] While JP 3-24's definition includes violence as a required operational element, this study posits that a nascent insurgency can be composed of those who have simply chosen not to recognize the legitimacy of a governing structure, and oppose that structure through nonviolent means. They may consider themselves patriots but refuse to involve themselves in the national political system due to a belief that all politicians are corrupt and unresponsive to their needs. At the same time, they may recognize the legitimacy of their local city government and continue to follow its ordinances and pay property taxes, but not the legitimacy of the factory where they work, and may establish a union to subvert its corrupt or exploitative management.

The essence of managing such legitimacy crises is not the tactical effort of finding and killing those who are blowing up pipelines and placing roadside bombs, rather it is the strategic identification of vulnerabilities undermining that legitimacy, addressing them, and thus preventing a need for violent insurgency to develop, which ultimately derails stabilization efforts. Effective and continual assessment of the environment is the key to consolidating gains in complex environments, and thus to avoiding the Stabilization Trap.

The Liberation Theology movement that swept Latin and South America in the mid- to late-twentieth century is one example of this kind of mainly nonviolent insurgency. The movement began as an effort to reconsider the Catholic Church's historical alignment with elites. Liberation Theology sought to refocus the Church on alleviating poverty by teaching literacy and empowering the poor by emphasizing free will over traditional fatalism that kept the class structure in place. Communities, often led by lay leaders, arose in remote areas that did not have a priest, ultimately numbering in the tens of thousands across the region by the early 1980s.

As higher Church leaders often viewed these lay leaders and communities as aligning with various Marxist movements, Pope John Paul II vehemently discouraged engagement in Liberation Theology, claiming its calls for revolution, while admirable for serving the poor, were anathema to

Catholic teaching, and certainly had implications for reducing the Church's own influence.[26] The first Polish pope and many others opposed to Communist expansion during the Cold War, saw Moscow's hand in the spread of this movement as a regional destabilizer in Latin America.

While Pope Benedict XVI publicly supported assisting the poor, he opposed the movement's "serious ideological deviations." In the 1980s, as Pope John Paul II's doctrine advisor, Pope Francis has since rehabilitated some of Liberation Theology's key leaders, and has emphasized helping the poor as his chief mission.[27] A cynic might suggest that perhaps Pope Francis sees expanding the Church's role to provide for those less fortunate as a way for the church to gain greater legitimacy with those still adhering to a Church with waning global influence and membership. In any case, this empowerment of local leaders who already have legitimacy strengthens the Mother Church by extension.

Some such groups see the state's governance vulnerabilities on a daily basis and know how to exploit them for their own ends in dealing with populations at risk. The Taliban had a similar origin. Fifty students under Mohammed Mullah Omar set out to alleviate the suffering of Afghans controlled by warlords, whom the Taliban considered to have failed to adhere to Islamic principles.[28] Understanding how to mobilize such nascent insurgencies, rather than ignoring or repressing them, can lead them to support state stability, thus avoiding frustrated violence.

A high-risk environment is one with an absence of stable governance, which lies along the construct of the legitimacy continuum. One does not either have stable governance or not have it. Much like a good marriage, it must be nurtured; neither a government nor a marriage will survive without that foundation of trust, which in society is called legitimacy. Focusing on those governed and their likely actions when their personal or community cost-benefit calculation determines that the risks of the status quo have become too high, David Kilcullen has identified seven survival strategies of at-risk populations:

- **Fleeing**: escape, which is easier for some populations than for others
- **Passivity**: extreme reluctance to take any action, typically due to trauma
- **Autarky**: armed honor-based populations refusing to flee or surrender
- **Hedging**: supporting all sides at once to "hedge" options
- **Swinging**: switching sides as the perceptions of risks change
- **Commitment**: committing fully to one side for protection
- **Self-arming**: becoming an armed partisan for one side in a conflict[29]

This calculation changes the nature of the transactional relationship from, "I support the government because it provides goods and services" to "I support the government because it will otherwise cause me to suffer." In the second instance, coercion has to become more overt for maintaining control over the population in the longer term.[30] In addition to Kilcullen's survival strategies, another that some at-risk populations might consider is formation of an alternative governance structure that views the state as essentially legitimate but prefers to control their immediate environment to the greatest extent possible. Obvious US examples are the Pennsylvania Dutch (Amish) and Native American populations in the US.

These structures are able to maintain the essential elements of their alternative governance when it does not come into conflict with the interests of the state. Some of these structures prefer to work *within* the state structure to address grievances and to resolve conflict; in this way, they are *legal insurgencies*. Although the military typically only pays attention to insurgents when their actions affect the states' interests, the most recent (2012) official version of the *US Army Doctrine Reference Publication on Stability (ADRP 3-07)*, describes insurgents with a nuance that does not require them to be violent, "Insurgents try to persuade the populace to accept the insurgents' goals or force political change. When persuasion does not work, insurgents use other methods to achieve their goals."[31]

Calling Evo Morale's 2005 election as Bolivian President a socialist revolution consisting of strategically applied violence, but mainly of nonviolent insurgent activity that began ten years earlier, David Spencer and Hugo Acha Melgar point out plainly in their 2017 study that

> Since insurgency and counterinsurgency have largely been a military concern in the West, dealing with the non-military side of insurgency is precisely where Western nations are weak. We have built very sophisticated military capabilities to defeat irregular military forces, but the same sophistication does not exist in the non-military arena. There is certainly theoretical understanding of the need for this non-military struggle, but implementation has been severely lacking perhaps due to the military's sub-optimal preparation for this mission and the civilian agencies' lack of consciousness and incentives to perform this task. Without completely discarding the military struggle, it is into this gap that new forms of insurgency are stepping.[32]

Thus, it is not only violent militants in Kilcullen's *Autarky* or *Self-arming* categories that are insurgents, but those in the *Passivity*, *Hedging*, and *Swinging* categories who, to ensure their own interests are served, are without concern for, or are in more subtle opposition to the state. Although typically only noticed when they become violent and disruptive to stable governance, their nonviolent actions can be equally disruptive.

One example of these is the Seneca, a sub-tribe of the Iroquois Nation located mainly in Western New York State. US President George Washington granted the Seneca 30,000 acres in perpetuity in 1791 for their assistance in halting the violent Iroquois insurgency against the US.[33] In the 1930s, New York State developed a plan to seize one-third of Seneca land to build a dam that would protect Pittsburgh from extreme flooding and provide hydroelectric power and tourism revenue for the state. The Seneca Nation waged a 30-year legal battle with lawsuits, engineering studies, Congressional testimony, and a direct appeal to President John F. Kennedy. Ultimately, however, the State forced 600 Seneca to relocate in 1962 to watch the "Lake of Betrayal," more commonly referred to as the Allegheny Reservoir, destroy their homes, and inundate their land.[34]

The State eventually gave the Seneca Nation nearly $16 million to build homes, a school, and other amenities to create a new town, and the government relocated their cemetery and delivered some basic infrastructure.[35] The Seneca Nation administers the Allegheny Casino in Salamanca, New York, as well as several untaxed gas stations, cigarette outlets, and other regional business enterprises. Their official website states, "Today, the Seneca Nation of Indians has a population of over 8,000 enrolled members. We are the fifth-largest employer in Western New York, creating thousands of new jobs and investing hundreds of millions of dollars to bolster the region's and New York State's economy."[36] Thus, the Seneca Nation claims to have ultimately gained economically, resulting in a return to stable governance in its portion of New York State. By peacefully giving up one-third of its promised ancestral land, it maintained two thirds and other concessions from the state, winning its legal insurgency.

There have since been intermittent acts of rebellion when the Seneca have felt their rights are not respected, such as in 1992, when 13 Seneca closed a 31-mile section of the New York Thruway with debris and tire fires to protest the state's planned imposition of a tax on cigarettes and gasoline sold by reservation outlets to non-Native Americans. The several-hours-long skirmish injured two New York State police troopers.[37] More recently, in March 2018, the Seneca owner of cigarette outlet decided to build his own off-ramp from the New York Thruway leading directly to his shop after losing a long legal battle with the State of New York.[38] It is important for the state (in whatever form it takes) to pay attention to such insurgencies to ensure local grievances are addressed before they become more violent or destabilizing than the events of 1992.

Alternative governance structures may fail to consider the legitimacy of the state as they work through faith-, ethnic-, or other affinity-based organizations to ensure their constituents receive needed services in the absence of what those states typically provide. Such structures may thus coopt the state's legitimacy, so that even while still nonviolent, their activities may result in instability. By the same token, a key differentiator of legal insurgencies is that as they do come into conflict with the interests of the state at times, but when there are mechanisms in place to mediate differences and come to an agreement, violence is less likely, even when the supremacy of the state governance ultimately wins out. This nascent power of a population to undermine stable governance is a kind of *invisible vulnerability* to state legitimacy.

The work of James C. Scott focused on Southeast Asian peasants' societal risk. Scott clearly explained that marginalized populations living in subsistence conditions already on the edge, whether they are rural farmers or urban workers, have such an immediate risk to their livelihoods, families, and existence that their risk tolerance is near zero. These populations will always strive to reduce or avoid risk to themselves, perhaps using the manipulation methods described by Kilcullen or others, to ensure predictability and reduce outside influence that can destabilize their precarious existence. Such perceived risks can include the efforts of their own governments, even if they would result in long-term gains,[39] such as insurgencies targeting new farming methods or forced moves from slums or housing projects to new accommodations, even when these changes would have overall positive effects.

State-centric approaches may cause a population to gravitate toward a neo-feudal relationship with a member of the local elite or a criminal gang that can keep the threatening action from reducing predictability and increasing perceived risk, even if this means dependence and exploitation by the stronger partner. Those who study insurgency or practice stabilization, such as analysts, often misunderstand that the underclass sometimes *chooses* their circumstance due to a relationship that provides clear incentives.[40] Policymakers in democracies are personally unlikely to face such choices as the ballot box, not the gun, is the path to achieving competitive control[41] in their world.

NOTES

1. *Guiding Principles for Stabilization and Reconstruction*, United States Institute of Peace and U.S. Army Peace Keeping and Stability Operations Institute, 2009, pp. 8–98. Available from https://www.usip.org/sites/default/files/guiding_principles_full.pdf accessed on January 4, 2018.
2. Rachel Gisselquist, "What Does "Good Governance" Mean?" United Nations University website, February 9, 2012. Available from https://unu.edu/publications/articles/what-does-good-governance-mean.html accessed on May 1, 2018.
3. *Guiding Principles for Stabilization and Reconstruction*, United States Institute of Peace and U.S. Army Peace Keeping and Stability Operations Institute, 2009, pp. 8–98. Available from https://www.usip.org/sites/default/files/guiding_principles_full.pdf accessed on May 1, 2018.
4. *Guiding Principles for Stabilization and Reconstruction*, United States Institute of Peace and U.S. Army Peace Keeping and Stability Operations Institute, 2009, pp. 3–17. Available from https://www.usip.org/sites/default/files/guiding_principles_full.pdf accessed on May 1, 2018.
5. *Guiding Principles for Stabilization and Reconstruction*, United States Institute of Peace and U.S. Army Peace Keeping and Stability Operations Institute, 2009, pp. 7–88–89. Available from https://www.usip.org/sites/default/files/guiding_principles_full.pdf accessed on May 1, 2018.
6. *Guiding Principles for Stabilization and Reconstruction*, United States Institute of Peace and U.S. Army Peace Keeping and Stability Operations Institute, 2009, pp. 8–107. Available from https://www.usip.org/sites/default/files/guiding_principles_full.pdf accessed on May 1, 2018. Original source: Beth Cole and Christina Caan, "Transitional Governance: From Bullets to Ballots," Washington, DC: United States Institute of Peace, 2006.
7. "Stabilization Assistance Review: A Framework for Maximizing the Effectiveness of U.S. Government Efforts to Stabilize Conflict-Affected Areas," p. 8. Released by U.S. government on June 18, 2018. Available from https://www.state.gov/r/pa/prs/ps/2018/06/283334.htm accessed on July 27, 2018.
8. David Kilcullen, *Out of the Mountains: The Coming Age of the Urban Guerrilla*, London, UK: Oxford University Press, 2013, p. 121.
9. Transcript of CNN's "ISIS – Blindsided: How 9/11 Created ISIS." Available from www.cnn.com/TRANSCRIPTS/1505/11/csr.01.html accessed July 20, 2015.
10. A.H. Maslow, "A theory of human motivation," *Psychological Review* 50 (4): pp. 370–96, accessible via http://psychclassics.yorku.ca/Maslow/motivation.htm accessed on March 22, 2018.

11. David Kilcullen, *Out of the Mountains: The Coming Age of the Urban Guerrilla*, London, UK: Oxford University Press, 2013, p. 123.
12. Transcript of CNN's "ISIS – Blindsided: How 9/11 Created ISIS." Available from www.cnn.com/TRANSCRIPTS/1505/11/csr.01.html accessed July 20, 2015.
13. Louise Wiuff Moe, "Addressing State Fragility in Africa: A Need to Challenge the Established 'Wisdom'?" in *FIIA Report* (Helsinki: The Finnish Institute of International Affairs, 2010), p. 31. Available from www.fiia.fi/assets/publications/UPI_FIIA22_Moe_web_080610.pdf accessed on March 29, 2018.
14. Moss, Todd J. (1995) "US Policy and Democratisation in Africa: The Limits of Liberal Universalism," *The Journal of Modern African Studies*, Vol. 33, No. 2 (Jun. 1995), (pp. 202–03) (pp. 205–06).
15. Quoted in U.S. Embassy Mogadishu, Somalia Press Release, "Winds of Change in Africa, June 7, 1990.
16. George F. Kennan, "Morality and Foreign Policy" in Foreign Affairs, Vol. 64, No. 2 (Winter 1985), pp. 209–10. Available from https://www.law.upenn.edu/live/files/5139-kennanmoralityandforeignpolicyforeignaffairswinter.pdf accessed on May 2, 2018.
17. Sudhir Venkatesh, *Gang Leader for a Day: A Rogue Sociologist Takes to the Streets*, New York, NY: Penguin Publishing, 2008.
18. Anastasia Angueletou-Marteau, "Informal water suppliers meeting water needs in the peri-urban territories of Mumbai, an Indian perspective," Laboratoire D'economie De La Production Et De L'integration Internationale, Note De Travail No. 20/2008. Available from https://halshs.archives-ouvertes.fr/halshs-00363464/documentrchives-ouvertes.fr/halshs-00363464/document accessed on March 22, 2018.
19. Coco McCabe, "Haiti's Entrepreneurs Keep Life Going Part II," *Huffington Post*, January 27, 2010. Available from https://www.huffingtonpost.com/coco-mcabe/haitis-entrepreneurs-keep_b_441769.html accessed on March 22, 2018.
20. This concept emerged through the author's discussion with LTC Joe Long in Crystal City, VA on 16, 2017 about his doctoral dissertation research on guerilla leadership and legitimacy.
21. *JP 3-20 Security Cooperation*, May 23, 2017. Available from http://www.jcs.mil/Doctrine/Joint-Doctrine-Pubs/3-0-Operations-Series/ accessed on March 28, 2018.
22. LTC Joseph Long, "Guerilla Leadership: A Strategic Guide to Developing Connection Through Guerilla Warfare," University of Charleston, unpublished draft white paper furnished to the author by LTC Long in December 2017, pp. 16–17.

23. *Joint Doctrine Publication 3-07 Stabilization*, p. B-1 in "Annex B Assessment Frameworks and the Assessment Process." Available from http://www.jcs.mil/Doctrine/Joint-Doctrine-Pubs/3-0-Operations-Series/ accessed on June 11, 2018.

24. Although *Joint Doctrine Publication 3-07 Stabilization*, p. 141, August 2016 states, "Many of the stability transitions cut across the political and functional areas. Planners should not consider these duties in isolation but be consistently cognizant of the possible effects their actions can have across both areas. This requires insight into the cultures of the HN, support from intelligence sources, collaboration with interorganizational stakeholders, and a thorough understanding of the desired political outcomes of the transition." Few commanders are truly equipped to develop these insights and recognition of the importance of the strategic objectives and how they relate to each engagement and mission task. Available from http://www.jcs.mil/Doctrine/Joint-Doctrine-Pubs/3-0-Operations-Series/ accessed on March 13, 2018.

   This common "mission accomplished, move on to the next objective," mindset within the military is contrastable with the long-term relationships generally built by special operations force units in AFG and elsewhere. This relationship pertaining to insurgencies is discussed in detail in LTC Joseph Long "Framing Indigenous Leadership," *Advances in Social Sciences Research Journal*, Vol. 4, No. 6, March 25, 2017.

25. U.S. Military Doctrine *Joint Publication on Counterinsurgency (JP 3-24)*, published November 22, 2013 P. GL-5. Available from www.jcs.mil/Portals/36/Documents/Doctrine/pubs/jp3_24.pdf accessed on May 1, 2018.

26. Olivia Singer, "Liberation Theology in Latin America," Web Supplement for *Modern Latin America*, 8th Edition, London, UK: Oxford University Press, 2013. Available from https://library.brown.edu/create/modernlatinamerica/chapters/chapter-15-culture-and-society/essays-on-culture-and-society/liberation-theology-in-latin-america/ accessed on March 29, 2018.

27. Stephanie Kirchgaessner and Johnathan Watts, "Catholic church warms to liberation theology as founder heads to Vatican," *The Guardian*, May 11, 2015. Available from https://www.theguardian.com/world/2015/may/11/vatican-new-chapter-liberation-theology-founder-gustavo-gutierrez accessed on May 1, 2018.

28. Kamal Matinuddin, *The Taliban Phenomenon, Afghanistan 1994–1997*, London, UK: Oxford University Press, 1999, pp. 17–23.

29. David Kilcullen, *Out of the Mountains: The Coming Age of the Urban Guerrilla*, London, UK: Oxford University Press, 2013, pp. 163–67.

30. Ibid.

31. U.S. Army Doctrine Reference Publication on Stability (ADRP 3-07), 2012. Available from https://armypubs.army.mil/epubs/DR_pubs/DR_a/pdf/web/adrp3_07.pdf accessed on July 11, 2018.
32. David E. Spencer & Hugo Acha Melgar "Bolivia, a new model insurgency for the twenty-first century: from Mao back to Lenin," *Small Wars & Insurgencies*, 2017, 28:3, pp. 629–60. Available from https://doi.org/10.1080/09592318.2017.1307617 accessed on May 21, 2018.
33. Letter from George Washington to the Seneca Chiefs, 19 January 1791. Available from https://founders.archives.gov/documents/Washington/05-07-02-0138 accessed on March 22, 2018.
34. See the documentary on Seneca Relocation and Kinzua Dam project "Lake of Betrayal," information. Available from https://www.visionmakermedia.org/films/lake-betrayal accessed on January 4, 2018.
35. Kamie Laih, "The Controversial Kinzua Dam," Summer 2008, part of the Pennsylvania State University *Center for the Book* program. Available from http://pabook2.libraries.psu.edu/palitmap/KinzuaDam.html accessed on March 22, 2018.
36. Documentary on Seneca Relocation and Kinzua Dam project information. Available from https://www.visionmakermedia.org/films/lake-betrayal accessed on January 4, 2018.
37. "Thruway reopened after violent Indian protest," report by Hamburg, NY United Press International (UPI) outlet on July 15, 1992. Available from https://www.upi.com/Archives/1992/07/16/Thruway-reopened-after-violent-Indian-protest/8678711259200/ accessed on May 16, 2017.
38. "Is a Seneca businessman really building a Thruway off ramp?" New story on Buffalo TV WGRZ airing on March 29, 2018. Available from https://www.wgrz.com/article/news/local/is-a-seneca-businessman-really-building-a-thruway-off-ramp/71-533274367 accessed on May 16, 2018.
39. James C. Scott, *Art of Not Being Governed: An Anarchist History of Upland Southeast Asia*, New Haven, CT: Yale University Press, 2010.
40. David Kilcullen, *Out of the Mountains: The Coming Age of the Urban Guerrilla*, London, UK: Oxford University Press, 2013, p. 161.
41. While typically attributed to David Kilcullen, this term actually originated with Bernard B. Fall, "The Theory and Practice of Insurgency and Counterinsurgency." *Naval War College Review*, Winter 1998, who noted "But the "kill" aspect, the military aspect, definitely always remained the minor aspect. The political, administrative, ideological aspect is the primary aspect. Everybody, of course, by definition, will seek a military solution to the insurgency problem, whereas by its very nature, the insurgency problem is military only in a secondary sense, and political, ideological, and administrative in a primary sense. Once we understand this, we will understand more of what is actually going on in Viet-Nam or in some of the other places affected by RW [revolutionary warfare]."

CHAPTER 2

The Stabilization Trap

Abstract As stabilization is surely one of those "wicked problems," whose dynamism causes it to evolve even as the solution is being identified, it is impossible here to determine what precise prescription should be applied to "fix" every insurgency or alternative governance structure that opposes or does not support the political framework for which Stabilizers advocate. There are some universal approaches that can be considered in tandem with in-depth, persistent assessments and deep knowledge of the historical, cultural, societal, economic, and political context of each area of interest.

Keywords Stabilization • Alternative governance • Legitimacy • Insurgency • Drone • Multi-domain battle

In order to conduct effective stabilization, it is critical to understand how alternative governance structures in the operational environment (OE) maintain control over their own structure as well as the population they seek to govern. This requires teasing out the attributes of a successful criminal, rebel, tribe, terrorist, or other group, that enable it to control territory and people that the central government has been unable to control. The issue of incentives may also be a critical aspect of what allows alternative governance to rise and maintain influence. Almost immediately after the US or other members of the international community commit themselves to stability operations, they land in the Stability Trap and

© The Author(s) 2020
D. E. Chido, *Strategic Intelligence and Civil Affairs to Understand Legitimacy and Insurgency,*
https://doi.org/10.1007/978-3-030-20977-3_2

become responsible for the well-being of a population.[1] This is certainly the case for occupation once post-invasion combat actions have ended and the "clean up" is underway, but can also occur in cases when the US or another entity, such as the United Nations (UN), is invited by the host nation to assist in quelling or preventing violence.

US policymakers' consistent oversimplification of the long-term stabilization process into a set of short-term tasks or objectives drastically reduces the likelihood of a sustainable outcome. Elite perception of governance and legitimacy in the host nation is unlikely to mirror the perception of those being governed, so the longevity of this stability depends upon the state understanding its own legitimacy vulnerabilities as perceived by the people and by developing and implementing a shared process of strengthening the whole society. Rarely are external policymakers prepared to plan for the long-term reconciliation process and rebuilding of state institutions in a fully inclusive manner that will heal relationships between post-conflict states and their societies.

In terms of international actors, such as the UN headquarters' staff that determines the mandate and makes the decision to embark on a stabilization mission, the process is also long term and relational. For the mission team on the ground and its Force Commander, the mission is composed of a series of short-term tasks designed to create a transactional effect, meet the objectives, complete the mission, and withdraw and, perhaps, prepare for transition to another force once the deployment term is ended, while the mission mandate is extended (indefinitely in some cases). It is unlikely that, within current mission constructs, these divergent perspectives are reconcilable, thus stabilization remains a complex, even intractable problem.

No matter who is leading the charge in fact or in perception, some elements of society will always be opposed to stabilization. These elements or *spoilers* have a nasty habit of interrupting the progress toward development of a Western-style democracy and capitalist economy. Spoilers range from groups of citizens unhappy with foreign intervention, indigenous ethnic or religious groups that feel marginalized by the stabilization process, illicit actors that prefer absence of rule of law to enable their activities to continue unobstructed, or foreign-supported insurgencies from within or without the region for whom stabilization and Westernization is not perceived to be in their interest. As an intervention continues, various population segments make determinations over time on whether they will support the stabilization effort. As most societies are not monolithic, there will also be other groups, some accurately called *spoilers*, others more neutral, all making the same calculated determinations on whether to go along with the process in terms of their own interests.

Such spoilers may not even fully support insurgent elements. As Kilcullen has described, in the case of those living under Taliban-control, for instance, in the mainly nonliterate remote regions of Afghanistan, an extended family may have occupied a particular piece of land for generations or centuries. They know it, their neighbors know it, but without a robust concept of private property rights and contract law spelling out land ownership, in times of danger, the family may be forced to flee and return to find their land occupied by an interloper, or a neighbor may try to encroach on this land. If the patriarch takes this grievance to the local Taliban commander and can make a compelling case, the commander will determine that the land is his and the dispute is settled. Perhaps this patriarch has good reason to oppose the Taliban in principle, but now must at least tacitly, and perhaps on occasion more fully, support its sustained presence, lest the land rights be contested under another regime less sympathetic to him.[2]

The indigenous people will remain (unless they flee too far and for too long), so for them, stabilization is a process. However, as in the case of Kilcullen's Hedgers and Swingers, the process and the long-term relational aspect is with the environment, natural and human. During stabilization, the population's behavior toward transactional stabilization actors will also be appropriately transactional, but their neighbors will remember their actions long after official stabilization operations are over, perhaps for centuries.

Spoilers may be indigenous or not, but for them, destabilization is a *task*; although managing what happens if they can gain control of the state, or other resource or territory of interest, is the next phase, and will be a *process*. However, this is not yet necessarily part of the spoilers' calculus. The dilemma for the stabilization actor, seen in Fig. 2.1 as a *trap*, whether in concert or competition with the occupied or host state, is how to ensure it can complete its planned stabilization tasks before losing support of the people and creating insurgencies of all types.

As illustrated in Fig. 2.1, both the Stabilizer (S) and the Alternative (A) have a basket of goods and services (G) to offer the Population (P), whose support (—) is the prize in the competition. These baskets will have varying appeal to the population, depending upon its changing needs over time, and its long- or short-term interests, as well as the understanding of those needs and desires by both the Stabilizer and the Alternative.

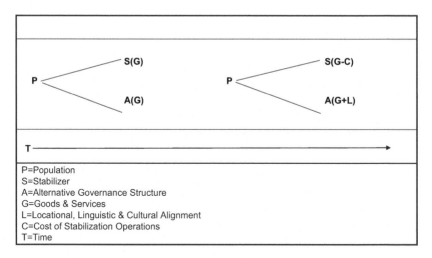

Fig. 2.1 The Stabilization Trap (Graphic designed by author)

The Stabilizer, however, has a definite and rising Cost (C) to maintain the process, which increases exponentially over time in terms of resources, personnel, and will. The Alternative has linguistic and cultural knowledge and possibly affinity on its side (L), which is a positive for it, as much as cost is a negative for the Stabilizer. The Alternative intends to stay as a positive locational aspect of (L), so Time (T) is less of a negative factor for it than for the Stabilizer, which only has as much time as its mandate allows, or its own population will support.

An external Stabilizer does not need much legitimacy. External forces are there to support the state and will leave once they accomplish the tasks assigned (short term, transactional). However, as its actions are intended to support the state, negative effects on the population will have long-term negative effects on the state's ability to achieve and maintain legitimacy, as the external Stabilizer is seen as the state's partner and thus, as a reflection of it. The state must have a long-term, relational attitude toward the environment, natural (and urban) and human, and must be careful not to destroy its relationship with either, while it competes for control in the short term and for legitimacy in the long term. As Colonel Steve Marr of the US Army's Peace Keeping and Stability Operations Institute (PKSOI) pointed out, "The state loses if it doesn't win. The insurgent (alternative) wins if it simply doesn't lose."[3]

Another important component of avoiding the Stabilization Trap is effectively managing expectations and maintaining clear communications in a format accessible to the target population.[4] Promising lasting peace and prosperity in general terms is likely to lead to mixed messaging from a population accustomed to being disappointed by government promises. Developing very specific tactical goals that can be accomplished in the short term will increase legitimacy, as long as the Stabilizer is able to take the credit. Relying on an active Twitter and Facebook presence in an area where people generally get their news in person in the marketplace creates a disconnect in which an adversary that knows how to communicate with the people can get ahead of the Stabilizer, claiming credit for positive outcomes and convincing people that unfortunate events are the fault of the intruder.

Managing Legitimacy to Avoid the Stabilization Trap

In the conceptual constructs of the Legitimacy Continuum and the Governance Hierarchy, the goals are two-fold. First, to move from the transactional form of legitimacy to the relational. This ensures that the governed trust those in charge will behave in a way that maintains stability beyond basic predictability, enabling rule of law institutions and infrastructure development, economic growth, and accessibility to quality healthcare and education, thus, laying the foundations for developing other elements of social well-being. These enable the society as a whole to flourish and remove the basic conditions of conflict.

Kilcullen argues that population control lies on a spectrum of legitimacy ranging from persuasion through administration to coercion.[5] Armed actors attempting to control a population of interest to them are likely to begin with coercion. This initially provides the type of predictability that ensures the population will prefer to remain under its control rather than flee or oppose its control. Beyond this, the alternative governance structure must then determine whether it has a long-term desire to remain the local authority, such as an ethnically based structure that seeks group cohesion and a permanent enclave of affinity within a state that persistently ignores or attacks it, like the Seneca Nation, since it laid down its arms in 1791. It could be a criminal gang needing to control the population surrounding a valuable resource, such as a mine it seeks to exploit, that requires the local population's labor until the resource runs out and the gang moves on.

The State Versus The Nation: The Case
of the United States of America

Debates on the concepts of State and Nation have filled entire libraries for centuries. As this study is meant to be a guide for practitioners, rather than a full-blown academic dissertation taking on the likes of Rousseau and Hobbes, this discussion will focus on the aspects of the "state" versus "nation" that pertain to the areas of stabilization and legitimacy in terms of alternative governance.

According to Ms. Tamara Fitzgerald, PKSOI's Senior State Department Advisor in 2018, "It is possible to build a *state* by establishing all the institutions (the Fatherland part), but you cannot build a *nation*, as this is born organically and is the essence of identity and unity (the Motherland part)."[6] One could argue that is how the American identity was born. An anti-British insurgency had a political need for a "United States," a transactional state-level unit buildable in the short term, but the concept of "America" as a nation has been a work in progress for nearly 300 years. The nation was once utterly rent by a bloody Civil War. Although a century and a half have passed in relative peace, there is still disagreement today on whether the state is inviolable or predestined for ultimate dissolution into regionalism without a fuller commitment to American nationalism, which often equates itself with historical and global *exceptionalism* to which some accede and to which others *take* exception.

As historians cringe over this simplistic version of highly complex events describing the US' own history as insurgent leaders, initially persuading inhabitants of the colonies to join the independence side in deed or at least in spirit, essentially on a shared perception of an unfair economic system that exploited the colonies without providing sufficient return. After the conflict, the insurgents eventually became the legitimate leaders of the new state and persuaded the militias that had once united to fight the shared enemy and intended to melt back to their towns and farms Cincinnatus-style, to instead share in a federated administration.

Once the British had been defeated, noncombatant loyalists had then to decide whether to continue the armed opposition without the crown's support, flee to England, or join the new state now under elected, rather than monarchical rule. Persistent discussion of first British, then French (now Russian!), potential meddling in US domestic affairs began the process of "nationalizing" the states and their constituents and militias into a common defensive posture against a perceived, shared, and now perpetually redefined external threat.

The Constitutional Conventions established early administrative legitimacy and the adoption of new laws and jurisdictions that have proceeded to become increasingly complex. Through mainly inclusive and consistent policies and institutions, political campaigning and elections, protection of basic freedoms, and through conjoining cultural expressions and transparent regulations, these laws have now largely been evenly applied and embedded in the national psyche. Such transparency makes it easier for people to follow this "normative system" with predictability through clear penalties for opposing the system, and legal methods for changing it.[7]

In addition to the consultative process at the national and state levels by which members of the executive and legislative branches of this system are meant to communicate clearly and often with their constituents, they are to serve as loyal opponents of the other party, competing nonviolently for control of policy directions. The government also claims full control over the legitimate exercise of violence in the forms of the police and military, which it can call into action if the population, or segments of it, break laws and threaten public order.

Recent cases of coercive control include the 1968 use of the National Guard to put down violent anti-Vietnam War protests and the 1993 storming of the Branch Davidian compound in Waco, Texas. The Civil and Indian Wars are the most significant examples of the US government using coercion internally, which finally gave way to established legitimacy over an expanding territory and population for the next 160 years. Through the two World Wars, and the amplification of national symbols and rituals, the state established a shared American *national* identity, bolstered by common opposition to Nazism and then Communism, which thus galvanized Capitalism and Democracy as "American" ideologies.

Kilcullen noted that a society is likely to be more resilient if its governing structure employs all the elements of control in a flexible manner.[8] This is how the US has managed nearly three centuries of overall stability. Despite the unsettling attacks in 1941, 2001, and other destabilizing efforts by domestic and foreign state and non-state actors, contemporary threats to this system are likely to come mainly from would-be state alternatives, armed or not, who seek to undermine the global order that has allowed the US to become the most powerful nation both militarily and economically. Another potential threat consists of internal elements, who feel that a minority of elites, or corrupt individuals, or corporate interests, have subverted the system through politics, and that the system no longer functions on behalf of the governed.

Researchers on these topics often begin by asking why people join insurgencies. This may not be the right question, as even the concept of "joining" an insurgency is nebulous. Those that have been used by insurgent groups as human shields to protect their hideout from bombing, or those whose villages and populations have been overrun by violent actors and forced to provide for their needs, have no official membership cards. In addition, rural and developing locales are likely to rely heavily on extended kinship ties for long-term, even generational, cooperation that transcends external conflict to ensure safety and survival in difficult environments. Identifying these long strands through social network analysis can be useful but can also inaccurately identify a person who has a tribal or other tenuous connection to someone on a list, who ends up targeted as a "terrorist" himself, just by calling that relative on a cell phone.

LEGITIMACY AND COMPLEXITY

A still-evolving Army concept of the operational environment being "multi-domain" is intended to describe how the military should operate against more capable and technologically enabled adversaries in an increasingly complex and multi-polar world. The multi-domain viewpoint is essentially a new description, with a healthy dose of concern over technological change and skewed collective historical memory that the world is now so complex that World War II and the subsequent Cold War appear in hindsight like isolated duels of giants. This multi-domain perspective suggests policymakers have forgotten the long history of feudal complexity, marauding knights, outlaws, and state-sponsored troubadours collecting intelligence and spreading real and fake news around the countryside.

In reality, the political backdrop of all battlefields has always been complex and composed of many far-ranging conflicts, consisting not only of tidy rows of soldiers facing one another across a field, but also of ideas, perceptions, and political objectives rooted in international relations. Despite the technological advances, "new" elements appear to make today's operational environment unique, but this complexity has always existed, new technology aside.[9] The technological advancement of one adversary over another and the use of one's own assets against oneself, as in cyberwar, are not new phenomena. Historical parallels abound such as the use of proxy forces (French partisans as saboteurs), drones (carrier pigeons), fake news (Soviet and satellite disinformation campaigns), election meddling (Chilean President Salvador Allende's and Iranian Prime

Minister Mohammed Mosaddegh's overthrows), and electronic signals warfare (cracking enigma and continuing to use its codes against the Nazis). From the strategic perspective, recognition of the perpetual complexity of the environment is *all* that should be needed to align appropriate assets to understand and manage it. The new Joint Concept for Integrated Campaigning (JCIC) is relevant here and may even be new as its foundational idea is to provide an "expanded view of the operating environment by proposing the notion of a competition continuum ... offering an alternative to the obsolete peace/war binary with a new model of cooperation, competition below armed conflict, and armed conflict ... not mutually exclusive conditions ... but states of relationships with other actors that can exist concurrently."[10]

This is where intelligence analysis, Civil Affairs, and information operations are critical to ensuring the military has a shared understanding of the environment and is working through all US instruments of power (DIME: Diplomatic, Intelligence, Military, Economic)[11] to maintain this awareness and use it to ensure legitimacy of the mission and the host nation. Otherwise, it will lose the support of the people and their shifting perceptions of legitimacy as a larger concept, as well as that of alternative governance structures that may initially have supported or been neutral to an intervention but can quickly head for the spoiler camp if things are not going their way.

It is critical that the military fully understand how technology has changed the strategic planner, as well as the individual operator's ability to effectively fill their roles, particularly in fragile environments. As Andrew Cockburn described the rise of the counterinsurgency killing machine, first the strategy was devised to remove the head of a network as grounds for assassinating Adolf Hitler, assuming this would cause his adherents to dissipate and become normal Germans again. Then, it was revived in the US "War on Drugs" in the 1970s with the goal of taking out the kingpins, such as Colombian cocaine cartel leader Pablo Escobar.

Despite mounting evidence that destroying the cartels' leadership spawned more heinous criminal funding mechanisms, such as contract killings and kidnappings for ransom, when the more violent "number twos" became the new *jeffes* and created violent turf wars among the remaining smaller gangs, actually increasing the supply rather than disrupting it, the strategy was reinvigorated into the hunt for Osama Bin Laden in the mid-1990s. After the 9/11 attacks, the strategy became an all-consuming budgetary beast with thousands of analysts tasked to create and track a seemingly infinite number of "high-value targets (HVTs)." This even changed the lexicon of the intelligence community from the noun "target" meaning *a group or phenomenon of interest worthy of increased study* to a verb meaning *seek and destroy a specified individual.*[12]

One prime example of the overreliance on technology as a strategy occurred in September 2010 when a US Special Forces unit erroneously targeted a cell phone believed to be that of a "Taliban terrorist" in Takhar Province in Afghanistan. The man was member of the Islamic Movement of Uzbekistan (IMU), serving as part of the Taliban's political Parliament in exile in Pakistan. He was a relative moderate, who simply hated the Afghan warlords that the US had propped up in his region and hoped that he could be part of a peaceful political solution once the fighting had stopped. A drone strike killed ten people only tangentially connected to the Uzbek, while he was campaigning for a relative participating in the US-led efforts to foster democracy by running for office in Afghanistan. This unfortunate event occurred due to a cell phone SIM card mix-up and Special Forces failing to differentiate friend or neutral from foe in that environment. One of those tracking the Uzbek later admitted that a moderate ultimately willing to work with the Afghan government to address legitimate grievances might not be the most appropriate candidate for a "kill" list.[13]

As James Cooney, Governance Analyst with PKSOI argued in a 2017 post for the Army War College's *War Room,* "while President Obama has argued that drones are far more discriminating than conventional weapons, and therefore save more innocent lives than the alternative. The unanswered (or unasked) question is, would the strikes ever occur without this unique capability?"[14] Perhaps not, but they are likely to continue and must take into account the cultural environment and not exacerbate grievances against the Stabilizer, as did a drone strike on assumed "terrorists" in February 2010 that killed 27 indigent Afghans driving in a convoy from Kandahar in Afghanistan to Iran seeking work.[15]

The likelihood of growing reliance on lethal drones as a key foreign policy tool became even more certain on March 6, 2019, when President Donald Trump revoked Section 3 of Executive Order 13732 enacted on July 1, 2016, as the "United States Policy on Pre- and Post-Strike Measures To Address Civilian Casualties in US Operations Involving the Use of Force,"[16] which required the Office of the Director of National Intelligence (ODNI) by May 1 each year, to release an "unclassified summary of the number of strikes undertaken by the United States Government against terrorist targets outside areas of active hostilities, as well as assessments of combatant and noncombatant deaths resulting from those strikes, among other information."[17] This reporting requirement and the subsequent public dissemination of each prior year's data was intended to reduce the number of drone strikes undertaken in noncombat zones and to severely curtail the Central Intelligence Agency's (CIA's) drone program in favor of depending more heavily on military-led strikes. The March 6 order allows the CIA essentially to strike with impunity in virtually any foreign locale it may choose.

NOTES

1. LTC Joseph Long "Framing Indigenous Leadership," *Advances in Social Sciences Research Journal*, Vol. 4, No. 6, March 25, 2017, p. 250. Available from https://scholar.google.com/citations?user=ljxJ5YMAAAAJ&hl=en accessed on February 9, 2018.
2. David Kilcullen, *Out of the Mountains: The Coming Age of the Urban Guerrilla*, London, UK: Oxford University Press, 2013, p. 125.
3. Comment from COL Steve Marr, Governance Advisor to PSKOI's Stability Operations Division, in April 25, 2018 peer review of this manuscript. COL Marr further noted, "The Army shouldn't 'do stability' out of altruism or as a way to work itself out of job. The objective of stability tasks for the military should be to ensure/preserve legitimacy for the long term integrated USG campaign, and by extension, the state we are supporting."
4. *Guiding Principles for Stabilization and Reconstruction*, United States Institute of Peace and U.S. Army Peace Keeping and Stability Operations Institute, 2009, pp. 3–18. Available from https://www.usip.org/sites/default/files/guiding_principles_full.pdf accessed on February 22, 2019.
5. David Kilcullen, *Out of the Mountains: The Coming Age of the Urban Guerrilla*, London, UK: Oxford University Press, 2013, p. 133.
6. Tamara Fitzgerald, "State-Building Versus Nation-Building: The Importance of Using the Correct Term," *PKSOI Journal*, U.S. Army Peace Keeping and Stability Operations Institute (PKSOI), November 27, 2018, pp. 13–17. Available from http://pksoi.armywarcollege.edu/default/assets/File/Peace_Stability_Journal_Special_Edition_Nov_2018_FINAL.pdf accessed on December 26, 2018.
7. David Kilcullen, *Out of the Mountains: The Coming Age of the Urban Guerrilla*, London, UK: Oxford University Press, 2013, p. 133.
8. David Kilcullen, *Out of the Mountains: The Coming Age of the Urban Guerrilla*, London, UK: Oxford University Press, 2013, p. 134.

9. COL Steve Marr, Governance Advisor to PSKOI's Stability Operations Division, credibly argued in his April 25, 2018 peer review of this manuscript, "I think technology is directly responsible for the proliferation of (and subsequent military/violent use of) the 'domains.' There was one domain (ground) until technology enabled the warship, two until technology enabled the bomber, and so on. This goes back to the changing character of war vs the nature of conflict. Similarly, I would argue there is no such thing as the 'Gerasimov Doctrine' in Russia—it's Soviet theory enabled by contemporary technology."

10. Joint Concept for Integrated Campaigning, March 16, 2018, p. vi. Available from http://www.jcs.mil/Portals/36/Documents/Doctrine/concepts/joint_concept_integrated_campaign.pdf?ver=2018-03-28-102833-257 accessed on July 27, 2018.

11. Commander Jeff Farlin, "Instruments of National Power: How America Earned Independence," *U.S. Army War College Strategic Research Paper*, May 2014. Available from http://publications.armywarcollege.edu/pubs/87.pdf accessed on February 26, 2019.

12. Andrew Cockburn, *Kill Chain: The Rise of the High-Tech Assassins*, New York, NY: Picador, 2015, pp. 93–117.

13. Kate Clark, "The Takhar Attack," *Afghanistan Analysts Network*, May 10, 2011. Available from https://www.afghanistan-analysts.org/publication/aan-papers/the-takhar-attack-targeted-killings-and-the-parallel-worlds-of-us-intelligence-and-afghanistan/ accessed on May 22, 2018.

14. Jim Cooney, "Drones and the Disruption of National Security Strategy," *The War Room*, U.S. Army War College Blog, December 1, 2017. Available from https://warroom.armywarcollege.edu/articles/attack-drones-unmanned-aircraft-disruption-national-security-strategy/ accessed on February 28, 2019.

15. Andrew Cockburn, *Kill Chain: The Rise of the High-Tech Assassins*, New York, NY: Picador, 2015, pp. 2–16.

16. President Barack Obama, "Executive Order – United States Policy on Pre- and Post-Strike Measures to Address Civilian Casualties in U.S. Operations Involving the Use of Force," July 1, 2016. Available from https://obamawhitehouse.archives.gov/the-press-office/2016/07/01/executive-order-united-states-policy-pre-and-post-strike-measures accessed on March 7, 2019.

17. President Donald J. Trump, "Executive Order on Revocation of Reporting Requirement," March 6, 2019. Available from https://www.whitehouse.gov/presidential-actions/executive-order-revocation-reporting-requirement/ accessed on March 8, 2019.

CHAPTER 3

Contemporary Vulnerabilities to Legitimacy

Abstract Whenever any governing authority fails to maintain the trust of its constituents, it essentially invites an alternative to step into the gap. Current literature on governance and legitimacy suggests the primary common factor that ensures popular support of authority in a given geographic location is trust, a belief in the consistent application of laws or expressed social mores across the territory. Vulnerabilities to legitimacy can be difficult to identify. This is where the true complexity lies. Lessons from lost legitimacy are rife in past insurgencies or alternative governance structures, or in coups and other attacks on nation states. The key to accurately identifying and analyzing these dynamics and getting ahead of them is in having a deep understanding of the grievances of the people joining an insurgency, opposing the host nation, or supporting the alternative governance structure.

Keywords Stabilization • Legitimacy • Corruption • Identity • Chauvinism • Insurgency

Whenever any governing authority fails to maintain the trust of its constituents, it essentially invites an alternative to step into the gap. A review of current literature on governance and legitimacy suggests the primary common factor that ensures popular support of authority in a given geographic location is trust. This does not mean agreement with the methods

© The Author(s) 2020
D. E. Chido, *Strategic Intelligence and Civil Affairs to Understand Legitimacy and Insurgency,*
https://doi.org/10.1007/978-3-030-20977-3_3

of governing but involves a belief in the consistent application of laws or expressed social mores across the territory (i.e., "truth, justice, and the American Way").

In order to move positively along the legitimacy continuum, the Stabilizer must identify the specific sources of trust that impart legitimacy to alternative governance structures and their leaders, whether benevolent, coercive, or something in between, to understand whether and how to coopt, support, or undermine that trust to enhance mission success once defined. These sources of trust can be tangible, such as obvious affinity among ethnic, religious, or other groups marginalized by the state. They can also be an isolated geographic territory (which can even exist within a city), perennially preyed upon by a criminal or other coercive group outside the ability or interest of the constituent state to liberate or support it. Other examples of tangible vulnerabilities to legitimacy include foreign intervention, state corruption, land disputes, and popular grievances.

THE TANGIBLES

Corruption

Numerous forms of corruption exacerbate conflict. Most obvious among them are organized criminal and other elements who raise profits through a "danger tax" or who simply find that unstable environments enhance their ability to operate and increase the value of some of their goods, including arms. Another, perhaps even more insidious type of operator is the "tenderpreneur," working behind the scenes to ensure the conflict continues as they secure legal contracts or tenders to provide security, uniforms, arms, and other goods and services legitimate forces need to stabilize or end the conflict.[1] Dr. Michael Dziedzic calls such support to conflict *criminalized power structures (CPS)*, as drivers of "war economies."[2] Even *JP 3-07* instructs stabilization operation planners to ask, "Who wins and who loses economically if peace prevails?"[3] Such an assessment will aid in identifying potential spoilers once peace begins to break out.

Corruption is often at the heart of the tangible reasons members might give for joining an insurgency. This is not just from a desire to usurp the resources and privileges accruing to a ruling group but also from a perception that these elites have no "natural" right to it (identity) or they are misusing it and have lost the right to rule. For instance, in Somalia, some al-Shabaab members joined in protest of the elite corruption and frustration at the failure of government to bring stability, especially the US-backed Transitional Government established in 2009, widely viewed as a US puppet. Al-Shabaab struck back against the political interference and more kinetic foreign intrusions[4] with a May 2014 bombing of a restaurant in Djibouti, accusing that country of being a "launching pad" for attacking Muslims.[5] Such complicity in directly supporting an unpopular leader further decreases the legitimacy of the state, as it clearly cannot run its own affairs without foreign interference, thus causing the Stabilizer to lose legitimacy, as it is increasingly associated with the corrupt and illegitimate state it has helped empower. As Dr. Todd Moss noted back in 1995 when the US government encounters unfamiliar forms of political authority, such as that often found in Africa, it is "not geared to deal well with such structures. Its inability to come to terms with Somali clans and the absurd assignment of the military to 'nationbuilding' are recent examples."[6]

Opposition to Foreign Influence

In many cases, those attempting to bring stability by helping to solve the legitimacy problem may actually BE the problem. This Heisenberg-revealed nature of stabilization alone presents a significant problem inherent in all such actions. When a host nation invites a Stabilizer onto its territory, there is already a restive population that will be averse to any reinforcements the state will engage to disrupt that population's activities or blunt its interests. Some will simply not appreciate the interference in domestic affairs; Emma Sky, Political Advisor to General Raymond Odierno in Iraq, quoted a local Iraqi leader as insisting, "Iraqis like foreigners. We just don't like being occupied!"[7]

A more serious example is Osama bin Laden's satisfaction with US aid in defeating the Soviet occupation of Afghanistan, but when the Americans declared their intentions to remain in the holy land of Saudi Arabia, his allegiance quickly switched. This tangible grievance was due entirely to his identity as a devout Muslim who did not want to see his country, which encompasses two of the holiest sites of Islam, sullied by the extended presence of non-Muslim foreigners, despite their potentially shared enemies. This issue drove him to redirect his efforts against the U.S, once the Soviets had left Afghanistan.

Outside meddling, however well-intentioned, is also likely to create suspicion among certain aspects of the target society about the Stabilizer's true intentions. Sky memorably described another interaction with the female military advisor to Iraqi Prime Minister Nouri al-Maliki, Dr. Basima Jadiri, who intimated that by 2007 many Iraqis had begun to believe that the US had not merely intended to depose Saddam Hussein but to ruin Iraq and create civil war. Once Sky was able to convince her that was not the case at all and agreed that the Coalition's true lack of coordination was shocking, Dr. Basima insisted, "How can a country that can put a man on the moon, not know what it is doing? How can the U.S. not have had a plan for Iraq after removing Saddam?"[8]

Despite the fact that there truly was no plan, and despite the fact that US forces are still fighting in Iraq, 15 years after declaring victory and 7 years after its official departure, the Army has now "moved on" from Iraq. A study of lessons identified to prevent errors made in Iraq commissioned by the Army in 2016 under the "Operation Iraqi Freedom Study Group," was only grudgingly published online in January 2019.[9] The funding for the dissemination of those lessons and what can be learned from them for future counterinsurgency planning and training has since been reallocated in the delusional belief that the US will no longer engage in such small-scale operations and will only conduct full-scale wars with near peers.[10] The same lack of foresight failed to identify and apply lessons from Vietnam as the book was simply closed on that chapter of US foreign policy and history. Perhaps the US defense establishment has decided it only wants to focus on the kinds of wars that look like World War II, a war it can say it won decisively. Unfortunately, conflict typically arises in inconvenient forms.

Outrage

Outrage often justifies an insurgency and can become an underlying catalyst usually triggered by a violent event, such as an atrocity or attack on a deeply held cultural symbol. Such an attack typically relates to an intangibly felt sense of one's identity being at risk. The difference is that, while identity is used to incite violence over time and relates to long historical memory, outrage is stoked by a current event or act.

Most often, the catalytic effect of outrage centers on a *first death*, the memory of whom a population reveres. Poet Dylan Thomas noted in 1946 "After the first death, there is no other."[11] Even Josef Stalin, widely considered an architect of genocide himself, stated, "The death of one man is a tragedy. The death of millions is a statistic."[12] *First death* imagery lends a sense of righteousness to the offensive attack and resulting killing spree, turning it into a necessary act of self-defense in the face of the ene-my's undeniable planned annihilation of the believed perpetrator. Examples of first deaths include the first Serbian fatality of the Balkan Wars, which occurred on March 9, 1991 during a demonstration in Belgrade, when a Serb police officer accidentally killed 18-year old stu-dent, Branivoje Milinković. His parents say he was only going to buy cas-sette tapes. However, he became a martyr in memory as later street demonstrations culminated in the laying of flowers on Milinković's grave, while celebrating the deaths of Muslims.[13]

The first death in the 1994 Rwandan genocide around which militant Hutus could rally was the assassination of Hutu President Juvénal Habyarimana. His plane was shot down on the evening of April 6, 1994, and the sound of the explosion over Kigali is believed to have served as a "starting gun." Hutu massacres of Tutsis began in the capital within hours.[14] More recently, the November 2010 death of Mohamed Bouazizi, the Tunisian fruit seller, who immolated himself to protest police harass-ment, sparked the Arab Spring.[15]

Specific Grievances[16]

At the center of most insurgent activity is the localized set of grievances that ultimately cause the eruption of conflict and prevent positive political solutions. Understanding these grievances, which may be rooted in land or water use rights or other economic issues, social discrimination by a majority "in" group by a perceived minority or "outgroup" or other tan-gible disputes, are the ultimate keys to something that may not feel at all like "victory" but achieved a sustainable compromise solution.[17]

While the actual leaders of an insurgency may have other ideological or profit motives for inciting violence, they will appeal to these grievances along with the intangibles to ensure they maintain the support of the people who may not share their ideological aims or their profits, in order for the insurgency not to face one of its own. This is where the local adver-sary has the locational, linguistic, and cultural alignment advantage over the Stabilizer in understanding the local population and its unique set of circumstances and concerns.

As the world's population urbanizes,[18] a new approach to understand-ing grievances, such as uneven service provision or access to financial opportunities of another sort, will require specialized study, once space or turf, perhaps, rather than land, is no longer a key contributor to conflict.

Concurrently, alternative governance structures addressing grievances by marginalized urban populations will be on the rise indefinitely, which along with global increases in inequality, are likely to lead to more frequent conflict in general, and in urban areas in particular, but on a less than full scale.

More remote rural areas also have their problems, especially those in mountainous or frontier areas, which have always been somewhat marginalized by national or provincial governments that often characterize them as "lawless" and their inhabitants as "outlaws," or those who reside outside the law.[19] These alternatively governed borderlands have historically spawned various separatist or criminal organizations that we call insurgents or *narcos* or *extremists*. Thus, we sustain what Scott MacEachern describes as "European ignorance of the socio-political structures of the region," leading to repeated stabilization operations stretching back to the Colonial powers, who "were never willing to invest the resources [and administrators] necessary to actually transport European Systems of territorial control."[20]

MacEachern further posits that "outlaws may cease to be bandits if their activities are recognized as being legal; as when they settle down and start behaving in ways that state elites find more comprehensible," as in his examples of the American government's attempts to turn "savage" natives into sedentary farmers and ranchers,[21] and the effort at disarmament, demobilization, and reintegration (DDR) just beginning in Colombia after 50 years of civil war.

Such borderlands are often the most complex of regions traditionally characterized as wild badlands of insurgency, smuggling, and feuding, such as the famed stories of the Hatfields and McCoys along the mountainous boundary between Kentucky and West Virginia in the US. In addition to a multigenerational violent feud, extended family members engaged in illegal production of alcohol (because its sale avoided taxation) and livestock theft. In a similar vein, MacEachern documents the history of a small frontier area around the Mandara Mountains on the Cameroon-Nigeria border that spawned Boko Haram. A traditional source of wealth and influence in that region was slave raiding and trading. Today, young men can get ahead by smuggling illicit goods like cheap gasoline or by setting up roadblocks to serve as a personal taxation or banditry business in such remote areas. These activities, which may also include kidnapping, are often considered legitimate exploitation of a state and elites that have traditionally ignored the needs of the common people.[22]

Reclaiming these borderlands and addressing their historical marginalization and unique grievances is a sizeable task for states seeking stabilization or full sovereignty. The "mobile state" program currently underway in Peru is one innovative approach that may have some success. The effort deploys staff from several government agencies to remote areas the state has neglected to provide basic medical care, salaries for teachers, and other services, such as the opportunity to register in public databases for identification cards in order to qualify for additional services. The idea is to strengthen the relationship between the local populace and the government to counter the potential of criminal or terrorist infiltration.[23]

THE INTANGIBLES[24]

Vulnerabilities to legitimacy can also be much less overt and difficult to identify. This is where the true complexity lies. Such attitudes or offenses can build up over time to become part of a population's shared narrative. These intangibles are often deeply rooted in human nature and a people's sense of identity, and will be more difficult to recognize, define, and understand. A charismatic figure, who well expresses an ideal to which the state itself is anathema, typically leads the emergence of an alternative governance structure that can usurp the authority of the state. Such structures sometimes require members to sign or utter oaths of allegiance and vows of secrecy to the leader or ideal as a way to express solidarity with the group. Once the structure amasses enough support to rival the existing political order, it is ready to challenge that order, not necessarily on a national or regional scale in all cases, but first typically at a local level.

Chauvinism

This study uses the term chauvinism in place of nationalism as it includes nationalism as one form of zealotry or extreme prejudice toward one's own cause or group. This term more effectively addresses the "ism" required for insurgencies to espouse or invent a cause to maintain adherents who share this form of impassioned bias. Typically, a person means *chauvinism* when referring to political nationalism used against those on another part of the political spectrum or Nativism, when it applies to the complexities of immigration, or religious radicalism, currently applied to Muslim-oriented insurgencies.

Philosopher Lawrence Cahoone asked, "What does belonging to a cultural tradition mean if it does not entail the judgment that one's culture is superior in some respects to others?"[25] As long as it does not lead to violence or even arrogance, most Americans would feel that this is a fair point to some degree. Cahoone proposed the idea of "thinness" and "thickness" of identity.[26] The more "thick" the identification is, the more exclusive it appears on a conceptual continuum. For example, American identification as citizens has been traditionally thin. It is valued above all else, but it does not preclude identification of its loyal citizens with a specific ethnic or other group. This is clear from the prevalence of such self-identifying labels as "African- or Jewish- or Italian-American, which by no means calls the individual's adherence to the tenets of citizenship into question ("as long as they pay their taxes," Cahoone quipped).

While it can be argued that Muslims living in countries such as France, which has a "thickly" perceived sense of citizenship, have intentionally marginalized themselves into ethnic and religious areas; French laws, institutions, and attitudes about who is and who is not "French" contribute to the separation of the two within society. Therefore, this sense of "otherness" contributes over time to an identity separate of *Frenchness*, even for those who may become French citizens. Such alienation is likely to lead to acts of civil disobedience, like the perceived 2006 cartoon attack on Mohammed as an identity symbol that resulted in Muslims rioting in the streets of Paris and many other cities, leaving an estimated 200 dead globally.[27]

Famed genocide scholar Erwin Staub described this phenomenon in nationalism, for instance, as arising partly from a "combination of superiority and self-doubt." This narcissistic manifestation aptly describes radical Islam's chauvinistic and often violent exhortations about the West desecrating holy Muslim lands and "keeping them down" since the heyday of the Islamic Caliphate. Staub further indicates that difficult life conditions often strengthen the influence of nationalism. "Chauvinism and nationalism, in general, can originate in the experiences of shared trauma, suffering, and humiliation, which are sources of self-doubt."[28] The mood of the immediate aftermath of 9/11 in the US clearly illustrated this phenomenon, when despite historical "thinness," nearly every car, home, and business suddenly displayed an American flag.

Continuing with the theme of ethnic nationalism as an example in his seminal work on "Crowds and Power," Elias Canetti noted that chauvinism (although he focused on nationalism) often arises as an effort to define oneself by having an interest only in one's own fellow believers and "indifference to all the rest. Its components are an unshakeable belief in the superiority of this one [idea], prophetic visions of unique greatness, and a peculiar mixture of moral and feral pretensions."[29] Although this is a typical basis of exclusivist ideology, associated not only with nationalism as it influences politics but equates with the approach of any chauvinistic motivation for insurgency. In the case of radical Islam, there are innumerable examples from its vast production of propaganda that express its own chauvinism, using historical imagery to emphasize the righteousness of its cause to the detriment of those it attacks, verbally or physically.

Identity evokes all the shared historical tradition discussed above, but nationalism has the added dimension of territory, which relates to deciphering the basic nature of conflict. As economists tell us, resources are finite and must be divided in some way. Harmony is achieved when this is done so that society believes that resources are divided equitably. When they are divided in a manner that appears arbitrary, or along divisive lines, cleavages can appear within the social fabric in myriad ways.

Crowd Power

Elias Canetti claimed that the modern concept of crowds originated with the older and smaller unit of "The Pack."[30] Yuval Noah Harari asserted in his 2011 book "Sapiens: A Brief History of Humankind," that since hunter-gatherer times, humans function best in groups no larger than about 150, as larger groups develop hierarchies and conflict.[31] Even in 1895, Gustave LeBon noted that homogeneous crowds are likely to operate like juries and justify criminal acts without sympathy.[32] In a 1978 study of crowds and riots, Sam Wright noted the innate fear of being outcast from the peer group, the village, even the family, by noting that, "The cry of 'Where do you stand?' can lead to a commitment crisis."[33]

Therefore, the behavior and movement of crowds is contagious, once joined, it is difficult to break from it and sometimes impossible not to move when and where it does. Within the individual member, it is even more difficult to break emotionally or psychically from the crowd, as its "rightness" seems above reconsideration by a mere single individual. No matter how unlike its members, a conscious crowd will transform into a homogeneous group and will act as no individual would in isolation. This is because the human desire for group identity is so ingrained that the stress and fear of going against the group can overpower the anxiety caused by contemplating wrongful action.

When those on the extremes of the political spectrum realize on some level that their position is not nuanced enough to be fair or entirely correct, they tend to prefer the company of those who reinforce their position rather than question it to avoid the discomfort arising from such cognitive dissonance. It is thus with crowds swayed toward violence, albeit to a far greater degree. This can help to explain how seemingly "normal" average citizens can become willing participants in heinous acts, fully assured that their insurgency and perceived offense is justified defense in the face of planned annihilation by the perceived enemy.

Crowds and group environments especially draw in those less accustomed to developed social interaction or debate and drive the whole toward a heightened emotional response and receptivity, sometimes out of all proportion to "normal" reaction to stimuli. This creates the impression of mobs driven into frenzy by a leader's exhortations, marauding with pitchforks and torches (of Tiki or other variety). It also explains the pleasure derived from chanting as one in a large group at political rallies, slogans that may seem entirely nonsensical to those in opposition.

An obvious example of such a demagogue is Islamic State's leader, Abu Bakr al-Baghdadi, who is described as "physically unremarkable, a man of medium height with thinning hair and a naturally thick beard.... But Baghdadi possessed a prophet's fierce conviction in destiny—the world's, as well as his own ... he could see a divine hand shaping events."[34] Such innate or practiced charismatic demagoguery has a distinct advantage in creating and sustaining legitimacy among insurgents, which Stabilizers must clearly understand to avoid clumsy attempts at disruption, cooption, coordination, or replication.

Identity

In order to recruit and maintain control of the alternative structure's own membership and any nonmember population in its grip, the structure uses propaganda to provide a set of images linked to events that clearly illustrate that target population's territory, way of life, and even its very identity is in peril from the state or the group it opposes. This incites the masses to join the struggle intellectually, although at a very low consciousness level, and to join it later financially or physically.

The success of this effort depends upon the structure's ability to discover and display the key concepts and images that will appeal directly to the most basic sense of self and most elemental fears. Perceptions of oneself as a member of one society or another, be it a family, a village, an ethnic group, or a nation, are essential components of an individual's sense of identity, their most precious asset. The effective structure will skillfully manipulate perceptions for a desired political outcome. It will also combine these fears with the "tangibles," as relevant to the circumstance to sustain adherence, such as real grievance(s) or a first death outrage.

Propaganda and effective use of current media are the primary instruments of turning an aggrieved population into a wall of indifference or an angry mob. Studies have identified three types of propaganda: *war mongering* is that used to incite armed conflict; *subversive* is that used to inflame conflicts within an existing political order or across borders; and *defamatory*, used to incite hatred, passion, and fear.[35] It is difficult to separate these types of propaganda in the case of insurgency, as agitators use all three together, with the first emphasized to initiate violence and the third to support legitimacy.

A good example of an insurgency using all three forms of such imagery began with Abu Musab al-Zarqawi, the leader of al Qaeda in Iraq, who in his 2004 letter pledging allegiance from Iraq to al Qaeda and Osama bin Laden, vowed to "with great fury, instill fear in the enemies of Islam … [and cleanse Muslim lands] of every infidel and wicked apostate."[36] Abu Bakr al-Baghdadi continued a similar narrative and enhanced the use of this imagery, as he picked up the ashes of that group after al-Zarqawi's death to form the Islamic State.

Rather than a gradual approach of undermining Middle Eastern governments, as had been al Qaeda's original approach, Baghdadi believed he could "raise the caliphate's ancient banner, and righteous Muslims would fall in line."[37] His Islamic and classical Arabic scholarship allowed him to interpret *sharia* and recite prayers in a traditional manner, which made him a leader in the US prison in Iraq, where he resided for most of 2004 until his unfortunate release.[38] It also helped that he was a member of the al-Bu Badri tribe that traced its ancestral lineage directly back to Mohammed.[39]

After brutally seizing Raqqa in Syria and Mosul in Iraq, Baghdadi made his first theatrical public appearance symbolically evoking just the right historical imagery on July 4, 2014 (no accident) in Mosul's Great Mosque, wearing a black robe and turban like Mohammed is described to have worn during his last sermon, climbing the steps to the pulpit slowly, as had the Prophet. Baghdadi's speech suggested he took the mantle of supreme leadership of this reborn Caliphate reluctantly (as Mohammed had claimed to do), but that all must obey him as the burden was divinely bestowed.

He exhorted his listeners in traditional language to arm themselves with weapons and faith in order to restore the Caliphate across the world as the "defenders of the religion and the guards of the land of Islam."[40]

How Legitimacy Is Lost

Individuals may "join" an insurgency when other strategies fail or through seduction by those discussed above. The outstanding question is why they leave. New members that do not join out of zealotry will enter into the group with some expectations and perhaps some trepidation. They will have a transactional relationship with the group at the outset, anticipating that there will be an exchange of some kind. In order to keep members, especially if an insurgency drags on for years or has few early successes, the source of legitimacy must become relational and personal for the adherents. Even a criminal gang can feel like a family and have a code of conduct that expresses solidarity with members who follow its rules.

Lessons from lost losing legitimacy are rife in past insurgencies or alternative governance structures, or in coups and other attacks on nation states. In Zimbabwe, for instance, President Robert Mugabe ruled since 1980, revered as a hero of the liberation struggle across Africa and at home, while he, his military veterans, and their successors looted the once prosperous country and brought it to its knees with rot from the inside. Decades of coercive rule were brought to a quiet end in 2018 when Mugabe was placed under house arrest and his power turned over to a military leader, who then proposed Mugabe's rival within his own party to return from exile and face election.

Observers will debate for years the moment when Mugabe's legitimacy was lost. Some will say it was clear his health at 94 was so poor his supporters could no longer literally prop him up. Others will say fear over his domineering wife seen as an outsider taking the reins at his seemingly imminent death was the catalyst. Still others will say that the dire economic situation caused by his avaricious henchmen finally hit the point where society may have turned on the ruling powers. The process of loss had actually been happening for over a decade at least, starting with a coercive power-sharing agreement in 2008. Understanding the moment when the tide is beginning to turn, not when it already has and the situation has already changed, is critical to understanding how to regain one's own legitimacy and how to undermine that of an adversary.

The key to accurately identifying and analyzing these dynamics and getting ahead of them is in having a deep understanding of the grievances of the people joining an insurgency, opposing the host nation, or supporting the alternative governance structure. Without this knowledge, *mirror imaging* will cause the Stabilizer to follow courses of action that make sense to it but may not be appropriate for that population. Thus, the Stabilizer may address a superficial popular demand, but not the root cause of the insurgency. In other cases, the Stabilizer may impose a solution the host nation assures will appeal to all, but only benefits the host nation government, which will ensure the insurgency will break out again or the alternative governance structure will endure.

Community attitudes toward crime, fault, punishment, and justice also affect the creation and maintenance of alternative governance. Identifying how a national structure runs counter to these attitudes can provide an opening to undermining or gradually changing how these structures evolve. In many places, as political "progress" takes place in directions seen as positive in the West, new laws may run counter to long-held mores, such as loyalty to one's ethnic group or tribe, family, religion, or region. This sense of obligation can cause persons in both the public and the private sectors to go against the law without concern or an internal sense of operating unethically.[41]

The element causing the backlash, such as infringement upon the country by foreigners, could be reduced or eliminated. The outrage could be seen to have been adequately avenged or the sense of identity or inequality may have been addressed by a more understanding government or reconciliation program, but in some cases, it may be the insurgency or alternative governance structure itself that becomes the odious and unwanted external influence or causes the solidarity- or fear-busting outrage.

In the case of al-Shabaab in Somalia, one defector, who turned spy for the Somali government, explained that he left the group because, "They were killing clerics. They were killing without consultation, it was just guys at the top deciding." Others have expressed their disgust for large-scale killing of civilians, especially the October 2017 bombing in Mogadishu that killed over 500 people.[42] Recently, 45 "mid- and high-level" al-Shabaab members have defected, 22 since January 2017.

Such disillusion with the movement or leadership can grow organically as the insurgency changes over time, or its true motives, such as profit, can become more apparent to the population from whom it seeks support. Once a critical mass of that population no longer believes the insurgency has the coercive means to control it or finds that its goals are no longer in alignment with theirs, the people reject it overtly or surreptitiously by aiding those fighting it, or they may stage an overthrow. In Botswana, when a traditional Botswana Chief lost legitimacy with his people, they would literally "vote with their feet" and move to another territory, leaving the deposed Chief alone with no one to govern![43]

While this loss of legitimacy can occur organically, as the insurgency changes over time or its actions belie its professed goals and allegiances, it is also possible to highlight its weaknesses or lack of devotion to the population's interests. This is a careful balancing act, however, that can easily backfire on the Stabilizer that does not have sufficient cultural acuity to understand the population it seeks to persuade. This is why close collaboration over time between key figures in the population and Civil Affairs and intelligence personnel must develop a sustainable relationship with the population in order to institute a reliable process to ensure the information flow is fully accurate as the situation is entirely fluid. This concept is often referred to as "owning the town," wherein nothing occurs without some element of the population informing the Civil Affairs or intelligence personnel.[44]

The Stabilizer also needs more than a tactical plan to turn a few defectors. Harmonie Toros, senior lecturer at the University of Kent, stresses the need for a strategic approach, "The strength is that it [defections] demonstrates to a certain degree that there are senior members of al-Shabaab [or any other group in play] who are not crazy radicals that we can talk to. The risk is if you pull all the moderates out, you only leave the ideologues."[45] Despite al-Shabaab's clan structure with an easy tipping point of too many respected leaders or extended family members killed without consultation, it is unlikely that this is unique to Somalia.

Exhaustion with the fighting, killing, and loss of sustainable, economic opportunity will also bring combatants to lay down their arms. However, without an effective peace settlement that addresses all grievances, this situation is likely to end up as a cease-fire and not a viable end to conflict. In the case of Colombia, 50 years of violent civil war and marauding by communists and narcoterrorists finally resulted in a peace treaty in August 2016. The exhausted population that wanted an end to the violence still rejected the original treaty in a referendum on October 2, 2016, as it could not abide amnesty for the aggressors who had perpetrated generations of atrocities, nor the failure of the treaty to settle land rights issues resulting from past violent seizure or forfeiture.[46]

Today, the process is going ahead, but the referendum revealed that Colombia's elites, who signed the initial treaty, did not understand the concerns of the people directly affected by the fighting. Although Colombia is not entirely out of the woods, once the nation had caught its breath, another insurgency was likely to have developed had the situation not been more fully addressed in subsequent agreements. With so many armed men with no other skills than providing security or perpetrating violence and smuggling illicit goods, the jury is still out on whether Colombia can effectively reintegrate them into society. The impending implosion of Venezuela and its borders flooded with refugees is not likely to strengthen Colombia's resilience post-conflict.

NOTES

1. Kalume Kazungu and Mohamed Ahmed, "Poor communication, low morale derail battle against Shabaab," Daily Nation (Kenya), January 28, 2018. Available from https://www.nation.co.ke/news/war-on-Shabaab-has-dragged-on-inthree-counties-/1056-4282534-8wi48hz/index.html accessed via OE Watch, a foreign news sampler by U.S. Foreign Military Studies Office, Volume 8, Issue #3, March 2018 on March 7, 2018.
2. Mike Dziedzic, ed. *Criminalized Power Structures: The Overlooked Enemies of Peace, Peace and Security in the twenty-first Century Series*, Alliance for Peacebuilding, Lanham, MD: Rowman & Littlefield, 2016.
3. *Joint Publication 3-07 Stability*, August 3, 2016, pp. III–9. Available from http://www.jcs.mil/Portals/36/Documents/Doctrine/pubs/jp3_07.pdf accessed on March 22, 2018.
4. This includes Special Operations targeting "high-value targets" assumed to be involved in international terrorism (information available from Jeremy Scahill's *Dirty Wars: The World is a Battlefield*, New York, NY: Nation Books, 2013), as well as international peacekeepers in the country under the umbrella of an African Union Mission in Somalia (AMISOM), information available from http://amisom-au.org/ accessed on May 17, 2018.
5. "BBC Somalia Country Timeline." Available from http://www.bbc.com/news/world-africa-14094632 accessed on March 22, 2018.
6. Todd J. Moss, "US Policy and Democratisation in Africa: The Limits of Liberal Universalism," *The Journal of Modern African Studies*, Vol. 33, No. 2 (Jun. 1995), pp. 206–07. Accessed on May 2, 2018.
7. Emma Sky, *The Unraveling: High Hopes and Missed Opportunities in Iraq*, New York, NY: PublicAffairs, 2015, p. 184.
8. Emma Sky, *The Unraveling: High Hopes and Missed Opportunities in Iraq*, New York, NY: PublicAffairs, 2015, p. 190.

9. COLs Joel D. Rayburn and Frank K. Sobchak et al. *The U.S. Army in the Iraq War, Volumes I & II*, U.S. Army War College, January 17, 2019. Available from https://publications.armywarcollege.edu/publication-detail.cfm?publicationID=3668 accessed on March 11, 2019.
10. Frank K. Sobchak, "The US Army Is Trying to Bury the Lessons of the Iraq War," Defense One, March 8, 2019. Available from https://www.defenseone.com/ideas/2019/03/us-army-trying-bury-lessons-iraq-war/155403/?oref=d-skybox accessed on March 11, 2019.
11. Thomas, Dylan. (1946). "A Refusal To Mourn The Death, By Fire, Of A Child In London." Available from http://www.poetryconnection.net/poets/Dylan_Thomas/1093 accessed April 16, 2018.
12. This may have been a response to Churchill at the Potsdam Conference in 1945. Available from http://www.dkosopedia.com/wiki/Joseph_Stalin#Stalin_as_a_theorist accessed April 16, 2018.
13. Malešič, Marjan. (May 1993). "The Role of the Mass Media in the Serbian-Croatian Conflict: August 1st 1991 to January 31st 1992," Psykologiskt Försvar, Rapport Nr. 164. Stockholm: Försvarsmedia, p. 64.
14. Geoffrey York and Judi Rever, "Seized Weapon Sheds Light on Mystery of Rwandan Genocide," *Globe and Mail*, latest update March 24, 2017. Available from https://www.theglobeandmail.com/news/world/seized-weapon-sheds-light-on-mystery-of-rwandan-genocide/article34125905/ accessed on March 22, 2018.
15. "The tragic life of a street vendor," Al Jazeera, January 20, 2011. Available from https://www.aljazeera.com/indepth/features/2011/01/201111684242518839.html accessed on March 28, 2018.
16. *Joint Publication 3-07 Stabilization*, August 2016 accurately encapsulates some of this information on sources of lost legitimacy as "motive" for insurgent violence on pages 17–18, "The motives for violence vary between individuals and communities, and between elites, combatants, and supporters. For a joint force conducting stability activities, it is important to distinguish between the root causes that made a society vulnerable to instability, and how those conditions were transformed into drivers of instability by established or aspiring elites. The existence of grievances does not automatically cause instability: poverty, unemployment, economic inequality, inadequate essential services, political marginalization, and repression are unfortunately commonplace, and exist in many places that are reasonably stable. It takes leaders to build a compelling narrative that links grievances to a political agenda. Those leaders use that narrative to mobilize support for some political purpose, including possibly undermining the government's ability to constrain their freedom of action. The narrative explains who is to blame for the grievances, how the grievances should be addressed and what the population should do. The success

of a narrative is based not only on the substance of its promises and threats, but how it is presented to the target audience. Successful narratives typically frame grievances in terms of an ethnic, religious, political, class, or geographic identity, emphasizing its marginalization by the HN government. The identity provides the symbols, myths, and historical references that are woven into the narrative to bolster its credibility and appeal. Those challenging the authority of the HN government consistently reinforce the credibility of their narrative through communication and propaganda of the deed."

Significantly, *JP 3-07* alludes to grievances that segments of the population may attempt to have addressed nonviolently on p. 18, "In many cases, opponents of the government do not immediately resort to violence, and the response of the HN government may determine whether a crisis is resolved through peaceful political processes or escalates. Responding appropriately requires the HN government to accurately distinguish between legitimate criticism and determined subversion. HN governments may default to heavy-handed repressive responses that drive moderates into alliances with extremist hardliners, deepening the instability and pushing the crisis towards open violence. Escalation often involves deliberate attacks by both sides on important civic institutions, and the disruption of the norms that help societies function, creating physical and psychological trauma for individuals, communities, and the nation as a whole that can hamper efforts to resolve the conflict." Unfortunately, JP 3-07 does not clearly define alternative governance and indicate when small-scale violence should be assessed and understood and to not have the automatic assumption be made that the Stabilizer is the intended target. Available from http://www.jcs.mil/Doctrine/Joint-Doctrine-Pubs/3-0-Operations-Series/ accessed on March 13, 2018.

17. Daniel Marston and Carter Malkasian, eds. *Counterinsurgency in Modern Warfare*, London, UK: Osprey Publishing, 2008, p. 17.
18. *Joint Operating Concept (JOE) 2035: The Joint Force in a Contested and Disordered World*, July 14, 2016, p. 11. Available from http://www.jcs.mil/Portals/36/Documents/Doctrine/concepts/joe_2035_july16.pdf?ver=2017-12-28-162059-917 accessed on March 7, 2018.
19. Scott MacEachern, *Searching for Boko Haram: A History of Violence in Central Africa*, New York, NY: Oxford University Press, 2018, p. 95.
20. Scott MacEachern, *Searching for Boko Haram: A History of Violence in Central Africa*, New York, NY: Oxford University Press, 2018, pp. 146–47.
21. Scott MacEachern, *Searching for Boko Haram: A History of Violence in Central Africa*, New York, NY: Oxford University Press, 2018, pp. 191, 201–04.

22. MacEachern skillfully describes the organizational structure and activities of these local criminals, called *coupeurs de route*, in his chapter "Kalashnikovs, Cell Phones, and Motorcycles," pp. 116–54.

23. Dr. R. Evan Ellis "New Developments in Organized Crime in Peru," *The Cipher Brief*, May 20, 2016. Available from https://www.thecipherbrief. com/column/strategic-view/new-developments-in-organized-crime-in-peru accessed on February 28, 2019.

24. This section is based on prior research conducted by the author for her 2006 Master's thesis on predicting genocide. That work is not copyrighted and is available via the Mercyhurst University Hammermill Library and the International Security Network website at https://www.files.ethz. ch/isn/30270/DCHIDO%20Thesis.pdf accessed on March 1, 2018.

25. Lawrence E. Cahoone, *Cultural Revolutions: Reason Versus Culture in Philosophy, Politics, and Jihad*, University Park, PA: The Pennsylvania State University Press, 2005, p. 23.

26. Lawrence E. Cahoone, *Cultural Revolutions: Reason Versus Culture in Philosophy, Politics, and Jihad*, University Park, PA: The Pennsylvania State University Press, 2005, p. 28.

27. "Prophet Mohammed cartoons controversy: timeline," *The Telegraph*, March 18, 2018. Available from https://www.telegraph.co.uk/news/ worldnews/europe/france/11341599/Prophet-Muhammad-cartoons- controversy-timeline.html accessed February 28, 2019. This article traces the origin of the cartoons through the 2006 global riots to the January 2015 killing of 12 at the *Charlie Hebdo* newspaper office in Paris and the attack on a Texas art museum holding a contest with 350 Mohammed cartoons submitted where the two gunmen were the only fatalities.

28. Ervin Staub, *The Roots of Evil: The Origins of Genocide and Other Group Violence*, New York: Cambridge University Press, 2002, p. 19.

29. Elias Canetti, *Crowds and Power*, New York, NY: The Continuum Publishing Corp., 1978, pp. 108–09.

30. Elias Canetti, *Crowds and Power*, New York, NY: The Continuum Publishing Corp., 1978, p. 93.

31. Yuval Noah Harari, *Sapiens: A Brief History of Humankind*, Oxford, UK: Vintage, 2011, p. 29.

32. LeBon, Gustave, *The Crowd: A Study of the Popular Mind*. Mineola, NY: Dover Publications, 2002, pp. 108–14.

33. Wright, Sam, *Crowds and Riots: A Study in Social Organization*, Sage Publications, 1978, pp. 121–22.

34. Joby Warrick, *Black Flags: The Rise of ISIS*, New York, NY: Doubleday, 2015, p. 244.

35. Research by Whitton, B. and A. Larsen. (1964). *Propaganda – Towards Disarmament in the War of Words*. New York: Oceana Publications, Inc.,

cited in Malešič, Marjan, "The Role of the Mass Media in the Serbian-Croatian Conflict: August 1st 1991 to January 31st 1992," May 1993, Psykologiskt Försvar, Rapport nr 164. Stockholm: Försvarsmedia, pp. 107–08.

36. Joby Warrick, *Black Flags: The Rise of ISIS*, New York, NY: Doubleday, 2015, p. 175.
37. Joby Warrick, *Black Flags: The Rise of ISIS*, New York, NY: Doubleday, 2015, p. 252.
38. Joby Warrick, *Black Flags: The Rise of ISIS*, New York, NY: Doubleday, 2015, p. 257.
39. Joby Warrick, *Black Flags: The Rise of ISIS*, New York, NY: Doubleday, 2015, p. 254.
40. Joby Warrick, *Black Flags: The Rise of ISIS*, New York, NY: Doubleday, 2015, pp. 304–05.
41. James C. Scott, *Comparative Political Corruption*, Englewood Cliffs, NJ: Prentice-Hall, 1972, pp. 10–13; Joseph Lapalombara, "Structural and Institutional Aspects of Corruption," *Social* Research, Vol. 61, Iss. 2, 1994, p. 329.
42. "Somalia lures defectors in new push against insurgents," by Katharine Houreld, *Reuters*, January 24, 2018. Available from https://af.reuters.com/article/africaTech/idAFKBN1FD0QW-OZATP accessed on January 24, 2018.
43. Anecdote told by U.S. Army War College International Fellow from Botswana, now Brigadier General Lingililani Joseph, during Security Sector Reform elective course taught by Dr. Raymond Millen in March 2016.
44. Comment made to the author by retired U.S. Intelligence officer on July 20, 2018 at Carlisle Barracks in Carlisle, Pennsylvania.
45. "Somalia lures defectors in new push against insurgents," by Katharine Houreld, *Reuters*, January 24, 2018. Available from https://af.reuters.com/article/africaTech/idAFKBN1FD0QW-OZATP accessed on January 24, 2018.
46. "Colombia referendum: Voters reject Farc [sic] peace deal," *BBC Latin American and Caribbean News*, August 24, 2016. Available from http://www.bbc.com/news/world-latin-america-37537252 accessed on November 8, 2016.

CHAPTER 4

Recommendations for Regaining Legitimacy

Abstract When policymakers determine that intervention to achieve stabilization is in the long-term national interest, they must ensure that those with the requisite skills and experience within the Civil Affairs and intelligence communities carefully study the conditions on the ground to truly understand the human geography, no matter how out of favor such a term may be. To gain that knowledge, a strategically poised Civil Affairs and strategic intelligence capability must persistently study these populations—how they think and why—before overt action is planned or executed.

Keywords Stabilization • Governance • Alternative governance • Legitimacy • Insurgency • Strategic intelligence • Civil Affairs

The most critical action toward ensuring long-term effective stabilization is viewing it as a process, not as a series of operations that may or may not be loosely connected to a strategic objective. Such a transactional approach to foreign policy writ large, but to stabilization in particular, is the singular key to its consistent failure. The relational approach requires a long-term strategic plan that will not change with the US elections or with changing political conditions in the host nation. The biggest mystery of all is how to achieve this, especially if the political objective truly has primacy.[1] US Ambassador to US Africa Command (AFRICOM) Alex Laskaris quipped

D. E. Chido, *Strategic Intelligence and Civil Affairs to Understand Legitimacy and Insurgency*, https://doi.org/10.1007/978-3-030-20977-3_4

in an August 2017 presentation at the Army War College that military legitimacy can be identified from a population's perspective in three basic areas, does it have (1) capacity, (2) will, and (3) "nonreprehensibility," defined by whether the population runs *toward* or *away from* its own security forces.[2]

Dr. Donovan Chau stated in his 2008 Strategic Studies Institute monograph on *US Counterterrorism in Sub-Saharan Africa*, "What should be borne in mind throughout, and is often lost in the US policymaking process, is that foreign governments and peoples do not often view the world according to Western liberal values, attitudes, and beliefs."[3] Dr. Jennifer Keister reiterated this statement in her December 2014 Cato Institute article, "*The Illusion of Chaos*," "The preference for Weberian rational-legal legitimacy, and the fact that the West finds such structures more readily understandable than many alternative authorities, may lead policymakers to choosing partners who excel at 'looking Western' rather than delivering results."[4] Despite the number of times this is referred to as a "lesson learned," it remains only a lesson *identified*.

The decisive victory of the coalition led by cleric and former militant Muktada al-Sadr in the May 2018 parliamentary election in Iraq is a clear manifestation of such a preference thwarted, as the US-preferred candidate came in third.[5] Sadr came to US attention during the early phase of the Iraq war as a staunch opponent to US occupation. As a member of a prominent Shi'a clerical family who opposed Saddam Hussein, his supporters formed the Mahdi Army militia group that violently attacked US troops as well as Sunni civilians. In 2008, he denounced violence and began organizing massive protests and civil unrest actions to demand US troops withdraw from Iraq.[6]

After the majority of US troops left Iraq in 2011, his popularity only grew as he called for opposition to corrupt Iraqi politicians and mobilized his followers to care for the poor and most vulnerable Shi'a in Iraqi society.[7] Due to these activities and the increasing corruption in Iraq (the country earned position 169 of 180 on the 2017 Corruption Perception Index),[8] as well as low voter turnout, Sadr's party, allied with Iraqi communists, garnered the most votes of any other single bloc, but not enough to control the government.

This is definitely not the "Western-style" candidate that the US would have chosen, but his appeal as a leader is unmistakable. Now al-Sadr must learn to transform his alternative governance structure into a mainstream and legitimate political party. Western Stabilizers must recognize that if they truly intend to foster democracy across the globe, they must respect the process and learn not only to put up with winners they may find distasteful but learn to work with them. Otherwise, by undermining them, they teach formerly violent insurgents that democracy is not for them, which can turn them back into spoilers with their adherents likely more radicalized against Western influence than ever. Hamas, after its 2005 defeat of Fatah in the Gaza Strip[9] and the Muslim Brotherhood in Egypt in 2012, are examples of past unpalatable electoral victories in which the West marginalized and undermined the winners.[10]

RECOMMENDATION 1: USE CIVIL AFFAIRS TO EVADE THE STABILIZATION TRAP

In her 2017 book, *War and the Art of Governance*, Dr. Nadia Schadlow demonstrated that despite the Army's reluctance to lead stabilization, it is the "only organization in each theater capable of restoring order and stability in the midst of ongoing combat, then, once combat wound down, the only institution with the personnel, organizational structure, and geographic reach to implement reforms throughout each country."[11] As General Lucius D. Clay also noted about post-World War II stabilization, there was nobody "of requisite size that would volunteer to take the job or would take it, except an army officer whom you could tell to take it."[12]

Within existing or emerging alternative governance structures, identifying norm-based legitimacy factors, such as reputation, trust, reciprocity, compliance enforcement, and self-regulation, can be keys to the effective communication of tactical or operational goals. In addition, the introduction of respected figures that will assist in attaining goals that are of US interest is a critical method of undermining coercive or other leadership whose objectives run counter to US interests. US Army Lieutenant Colonel Steve Lewis underscored this in an article from the 2018 Civil Affairs Symposium noting:

> The U.S. has yet to fully appreciate the role good governance can play for the *counterstate*: groups looking to replace the existing state. The counterstate can also apply the principles of good governance in order to protect vulnerable populations and disrupt the activities of belligerent states. Understanding the role of Civil Affairs to support counterstate governance activities as their interests align with those of the U.S. is thus critical to success in UW (unconventional warfare) waged in the gray zone.[13]

The March 11, 2014, *Department of Defense Directive (DoDD) 2000.13* dealt with the roles, responsibilities, and organization of Army Civil Affairs (CA), charging it with numerous support responsibilities, most relevant of which is to "support stability operations, including activities that establish civil security; provide support to governance."[14] The *Directive* further clarified that CA is to "support unified action by interacting and consulting with other government agencies, indigenous populations and institutions, intergovernmental organizations, non-governmental organizations, host nations, foreign nations, and the private sector to provide the capabilities needed for successful civil-military operations."[15] This mandate provides broad flexibility of maneuver and engagement for CA personnel operating in stabilization environments, describing the capabilities and value of the CA generalist in contrast to those trained to conduct military government. Army Civil Affairs Commandant Colonel Jay Liddick stated in his 2017 Strategic Research Paper for the US Army War College, "The activities and competencies of CA generalists allow the commander to understand and visualize how the civilian components of the operational environment affect their operations (e.g. understand local leader or populace grievances or concerns that undermine stability in an area)."[16]

As COL Liddick further explained, post-World War II deployments of CA personnel in stabilization environments have been uncoordinated, to say the least, with unsurprising results. The lack of capacity, training, unit cohesion, and clarity of mission has led commanders to doubt the value of CA in precisely the missions, where they should be most useful if they were optimally trained, organized, and utilized.[17] Finally, in 2006, the Army made CA an active duty branch at brigade, rather than battalion size.[18] COL Liddick stressed that

> The importance of these two steps is noteworthy. By making CA an active duty branch and increasing the number of active duty personnel, the Army created a pool of officers and non-commissioned officers more readily available to support active Army commanders and solely dedicated to learning and further developing the capability. However, creating an active duty branch takes time, and this act alone could not fix all problems with the Civil Affairs capability.[19]

In 2016, when the Army decided to eliminate one of only two remaining active duty CA brigades, Civil Affairs officers Major Arnel P. David and Major Clay Daniels passionately expressed dismay in a *Foreign Policy* column at the unfortunate US preference for overwhelming force and failure to prevent and manage conflict by preserving and honing the very skills CA offers.

> Humans matter more than hardware, and a network of complex relationships yield unparalleled opportunities to mobilize the masses to take collective action against complex problems.... Preventing and winning wars require constant, effective engagement, an understanding of the local political and cultural context, and a cohort of military professionals dedicated to employing the full range of national capabilities. That's not a job for just anyone.[20]

Although Army CA was already woefully understaffed, DoD decided that as of fiscal year 2018 (FY18), only one active component CA battalion would remain to support Army general-purpose forces. This essentially leaves the reserve CA, which, by its very nature, is not available at full capacity at all times and will be unable to perform most of its required functions including support to consolidating gains through securing and stabilizing fragile and post-conflict environments. This realignment also significantly curtails active CA officers' and noncommissioned officers' capability to contribute to strategic and operational planning.[21] There has to be a better way.

Even as the Army shortsightedly reduces this crucial branch, improvements within the remaining capacity can help ensure the value of every individual officer. Beginning with recruitment of the most suitable members of what should be considered an elite team, the Clausewitzean attribute of *coup d'oeil*, needs to be defined and metrics assigned to determine how to assess it among incoming soldiers and officers. Civil Affairs must be composed of "individuals at ease with ambiguity and possessing of that ability to grasp pith amidst chaff," as Dr. Russell W. Glenn, Deputy Chief of Staff of the US Army Training and Doctrine Command (TRADOC), described this attribute.[22]

ADRP 3-07 (2012 publication) also noted that, "Paramount to successful counterinsurgency operations are stability activities aimed at increasing *host-nation government legitimacy* by providing services and security to the local populace."[23] In terms of understanding the environment, the 2012 ADRP emphasizes intelligence for influencing the population, but does not mention Civil Affairs as a resource in this effort at all:

In operations emphasizing stability tasks, depth extends influence in time, space, purpose, and resources to affect the environment and conditions. In these operations, intelligence combined with inform and influence activities help commanders understand factional motives, identify power centers, and shape the environment. As commanders speak to many locals from many different perspectives, they derive effective intelligence from the most accurate understanding of the dynamics on the ground.[24]

In fact, the most current 2012 version of the publication only mentions CA once, stating, "Civil affairs personnel have a major role. In these operations, they work with and through host-nation agencies and other civilian organizations to enhance the host-nation government's legitimacy." The section continues to describe influencing and shaping activities only. The new version under review as of this writing expands upon the role of Civil Affairs and the criticality of it working closely with intelligence "to identify key influencers and understand societal fault lines and grievances, both relating to current operations and those that originally contributed to fragility or violence to ensure successful stabilization and that existing grievances are not exacerbated."[25] This provides a more nuanced approach to understanding the human environment and combining available skills to develop a Civil Preparation of the Environment, an approach that complements Intelligence Preparation of the Battlefield (IPB) with its traditional emphasis on threats, while the civil corollary should emphasize neutral observation and identification of opportunities with synthesis of both for comprehensive understanding and relationship-building. These things are true, as long as this language is maintained in the final version.

Many parties in conflict areas, including civil society and other nongovernmental organizations, as well as populations at risk, have concerns about the process of collecting information in order to conduct necessary "pre-conflict sensing,"[26] as it is often viewed as a sort of sinister intelligence targeting process.[27] However, it should be no more threatening (or classified!) than anthropological field research, or simply visiting the region, talking to people, reading their publications and social media, and forming some basic understanding of their influences, motivations, needs, and grievances. Such information gathering activity is of paramount importance *before* policymakers determine a need to operate in these environments without the necessary information critical to effective engagement for stabilization or any other intended outcome.

In Somalia, the struggle for stability has been ongoing since President Said Barre's government fell in 1991 with various actors gaining a foothold only to lose it. While Social Well-Being, translated into quality education, healthcare, and basic infrastructure development, is one of the *end states* envisioned in stabilization and reconstruction guidance, often it is impossible to provide these elements equitably without discrimination. A January 2018 article from the Kenyan *Daily Nation* about largely unreported small-scale but persistent al-Shabaab attacks on Kenyan towns on the Somali border illustrates the reasons why such understanding is critical in the stabilization process as the author states, "Most notably, the government has failed to deploy to these embattled regions personnel who understand the local culture and thus could foster important relationships, which lead to the residents sharing important information with the security forces. As a result, little in the way of key intelligence is being gathered through local contacts."[28]

While it is important to prioritize development and maintenance of basic infrastructure in all stabilization cases, fixing potholes on the roads on the Kenyan side of the Somali border may do the most to reduce instability there for a surprising reason. As motorists slow down to avoid these obstacles, al-Shabaab raiders ambush them and then slip back across the border. Enhancing security by simply fixing the roads may have a greater effect on Kenyan morale and support for the fight against regional instability. Unfortunately, the fight seems to drag on, increasing the financial and moral cost to the Stabilizer, as this slow bleed continues in a neighboring country.[29] The Stabilizer fails to recognize a potential "easy fix" to a growing cross-border insurgency fueled by its own ignorance.

RECOMMENDATION 2: REESTABLISH STRATEGIC INTELLIGENCE TO INFORM POLICY DEVELOPMENT

In order to understand the complexity of the legitimacy vulnerabilities inherent in every population and every state and region in which the US professes to have an interest is to take a longitudinal, strategic look at the world and determine whether the US wants to continue playing "whack-a mole" and branding all sorts of groups and people "terrorists." The military can continue to sweep them up in its patented targeting machine, thus likely spawning additional violent actors among their friends, extended family members, and admirers. Otherwise, policymakers must reconsider what the actual national interests are, then look around at the wider world and understand first, who shares those interests and who vehemently does not.

Somalia would be a place appropriate for assessing and adapting the campaign and its objectives. Once policymakers understand that Somalia is a loose collection of clans with fealty based on complex hereditary kinship relationships and that the country is currently three countries, at least one of which deserves recognition as an independent entity (Somaliland and possibly Puntland), the rump state could become a Federal entity. Under current international efforts, the failed governance imposition process attempted in the similarly historically configured Afghanistan is also failing in Somalia after over 10 years of external meddling, and nearly 30 years after the last autocratic centralized government fell.

Instead of installing central governments the populace does not support and spending millions per year independently and through the African Union (AU), the US has failed to counter the influence of Turkey and the United Arab Emirates (UAE) in Somalia, which are both more effectively training troops, but not enabling a "national" force the same way the US is. These countries are also making commercial investments in the country to enhance stability through economic development. Supporting recreation of an entrepreneur class to displace clan-based warlord, pirate, Islamic radical, and old elite influences is likely to have a greater long-term effect on stability than the current misguided effort to create "national" police and military forces under an alien constitution that does not support a looser confederacy of power sharing among clans. As Fareed Zakaria wrote in March 2019, "The dominant reality of Indian politics is its diversity…. This diversity has proved to be India's greatest strength as a democracy, ensuring that no one party gets too big for its boots."[30]

As alluded to by Rhode Island Senator, Jack Reed, in March 2018, "Twenty-five years ago getting off the airplane in Mogadishu, it was a complicated situation, and even back then, we said, 'Well the real key here is developing governance—the capacity to govern, to generate a sense of internal support by the people for their government. That is probably the best way to defeat any type of terrorist movement. We're still trying to find that."[31] It is likely that the Western-oriented international community will keep trying to find that until it shatters these biases and begins to understand the sources of legitimacy that can work together to make Somalia a functioning country able to provide its own form of governance and manage its own security and economy. These are noble goals but are they truly in the US strategic, long-term national interest?

Once US politicians make such sober, long-term, and realistic determinations, they must then identify what happens in the rest of the world. When the US involves itself in age-old sectarian animosities because the humanitarian impulse is to hinder the widespread killing of "noncombatants," aggressors see it and the international community as "the other," automatically complicit in compounding their grievances. Once the US recognizes that such intervention can often exacerbate conflict, it might begin developing truly strategic priorities with the understanding that shorter-term military actions may be detrimental to long-term stability or legitimacy.

One example of such a policy is the Commander's Emergency Response Program (CERP), which allowed field commanders to allocate funds to local reconstruction projects in Afghanistan and Iraq. Intended to provide short-term infrastructure development and employment, the Army also used it "as a tool for counterinsurgency (COIN). CERP funds were used to build goodwill between the people of Iraq and/or Afghanistan and the United States in an effort to gain their support in fighting the insurgency."[32] Widespread failure to understand the social environment resulted in funds that according to USID officials, in the case of Afghanistan, "were not always used for their intended purposes or in compliance with applicable laws."[33] The geographic distribution of funds tended also to favor restive areas, causing many Afghans to feel they had been "penalized for peace."[34] In addition to local resentments about resource allocation, there is evidence that not only did the funds generate revenue for the Taliban in the form of a tax on those who did work for the coalition, but also as a protection racket through Taliban intimidation and threats of violence against those who participated in CERP projects.[35]

When policymakers determine that intervention is in the long-term national interest, they must ensure that those with the requisite skills and experience within the Civil Affairs and intelligence communities carefully study the conditions on the ground to truly understand the human geography, no matter how out of favor such a term may be. This requires greater nuanced understanding far beyond the terrain, military capability of the known armed groups, resources, and routes. To gain that knowledge, a strategically poised Civil Affairs and intelligence capability must persistently study these populations, how they think and why, before overt action is planned or executed. This knowledge is, of course, also critical to have during stabilization, as noted in a 2014 study from the now defunct Center for Complex Operations (COO), "Consistent assessments of local conditions should be done to remain aware of changing conditions and minimize the possibility of being blindsided by unintended consequences."[36]

As Dr. Patterson suggested in her study on developing a School of Military Governance, the Army should resurrect the following skills for strategic intelligence analysts and this paper agrees and argues that Civil Affairs generalists ought to be trained in many of the same areas. Both occupations should also be encouraged to work with and learn from each other:

> Such specialization within the intelligence community could provide more nuanced advice to commanders both pre-conflict and post conflict in terms of how civil considerations may impact military operations, how resources might best be spent to influence portions of the population most at risk of returning to conflict, or who are the key power brokers with the potential for the greatest impact on the indigenous population. Such information would be invaluable to commanders trying to decipher whom to partner with in a given population.... A complimentary capability to the strategic intelligence function is the strategic plans and policy function.[37]

Dr. Schadlow quoted former Director of National Intelligence (DNI) Dennis Blair, in relation to Afghanistan specifically, but the observation can be broadly applied "The United States lacked intelligence about the power structures inside the country and other basic information." Schadlow continued,

> The U.S. did not even focus intelligence sufficiently to understand political competition for power and resources with which multiple groups, including many hostile to U.S. interests were engaged. Those competitions extended beyond the physical battleground and carried over into governmental institutions and security forces.[38]

CONCLUSION

The consistent folly of the US emphasis on *transactional* engagements over the longer-lasting, more effective relationship-building that requires an understanding of the context of the place and its people culturally, historically, politically, economically, and socially was on full display December 13, 2018 when National Security Adviser, John Bolton, announced the new US Africa Policy, which has three tenets:

1. Advancing US trade and commercial ties with nations across the region to the benefit of both the US and Africa
2. Countering the threat from Radical Islamic Terrorism and violent conflict
3. Ensuring that US taxpayer dollars for aid are used efficiently and effectively.[39]

While these sound reasonable, their entirely transactional nature belies the inherent US tit-for-tat approach to other nations that has always existed but is baldly articulated by the current US administration. When the Bush administration announced the creation of the new Africa-focused combatant command in 2007, it was largely seen on the continent as a Western effort to recolonize Africa and no state was willing to host it. The African audience viewed Africa Command's (AFRICOM's) mission as anti-terrorism first, securing oil reserves for US exploitation second, countering Chinese influence third, and with African interests much further down the priority list. The commander remained largely in Stuttgart, Germany, housed with his European Command colleague. A small contingent of US troops was deployed for brief rotations to a portion of Camp Lemonnier leased from France in Djibouti.

Today's far larger US footprint includes a permanent and fully staffed post in Djibouti, a new $1 billion drone base in Niger, among other, smaller bases and deployments, as well as joint postings with the United Nations (UN), the North Atlantic Treaty Organization (NATO), and the African Union (AU). A November 2018 *Military Times* report stated that there are 6000 US troops in nearly all 53 countries the Defense Department recognizes as "African" (this excludes Egypt, which the State Department does recognize as part of Africa.) As none of the Africa-based "terrorist" groups have threatened the US, their essentially localized nature with typical claims of allegiance to international groups such as al Qaeda and the Islamic State for their own aggrandizement is apparently lost on US policymakers.

In the case of Mali, for instance, the fall of Ghaddafi in 2011 led hundreds of Tuareg mercenaries, who had supported him, to return home to their traditional land of Azawad, a contiguous area encompassing land in

Algeria, Burkina Faso, Mali, and Niger. Better trained and equipped than
the Malian government's forces, the Tuaregs formed a secular, separatist
group, the Movement for the National Liberation of Azawad (MNLA) to
fight for independence of their region from the Malian state. They briefly
allied with some Islamist organizations having unclear ties to al Qaeda in
the Islamic Maghreb (AQIM) and were swiftly branded "terrorists" by the
Malian central government in Bamako. This got US attention and
"counter-terror" support was immediately deployed, despite the MNLA
vociferously claiming they had erred in allying with AQIM and were only
interested in independence, not *sharia* or a fight with the international
community.

Adding to the complexity of relations in this region, the native separatist Ansar al-Dine pro-*sharia* party in Mali refused to fight against the
MNLA or attack its strongholds to avoid harm to close tribes and kin.[40]
This left AQIM aligned with South American cocaine traffickers active in
West Africa, to do such "dirty work." This lack of shared motive divided
the elements fighting the Maghreb governments, leading to a messy
regional war exacerbated by the West's misunderstanding of varied separatist movements as a monolithic terrorist group. In 2013, the UN sent a
peace keeping force under the mandate of the Multidimensional Integrated
Stabilization Mission in Mali (MINUSMA), the name of which states the
nebulous aim is stabilization, as there is no peace to be kept. This international presence drew violent extremists to the region looking for targets of
opportunity to enhance their global reputation and spreading the conflict
as the drone base in Niger attests. The most prominent result of which was
the death of four US service personnel in October 2017,[41] thus the majority of the American public learned of such activity in Africa for the first
time, even ostensibly surprising members of Congress.[42]

Similarly, the case of the international community's reaction to the
extreme violence perpetrated by Boko Haram beginning in 2011 in north-
ern Nigeria, whose loose alliance with al Qaeda and the Islamic State networks is opportunistic. Violent groups claiming such fealty and appearing
part of something far larger than a local insurgency enhance their prestige
and recruitment capability. Sometimes these pledges of allegiance also
result in some training, funding, or access to a valuable supply chain, or
other useful support. In reality, these are disparate entities with deep geographic and cultural roots that make them unique nodes with varying
levels of shared goals and methods.

Thus, we internationalize local grievances and swell them beyond their true nature. If the US took the time to effectively apply its Civil Affairs and intelligence capabilities to understand the true sources of conflict and stopped crying "terror!" at every claim by local leaders, policymakers could more effectively determine the appropriate strategic approach, which, in most cases, is likely to be no approach at all. There is little reason for the might of the US military to intervene in hundreds of localized conflicts that have no intention or capability of threatening the homeland or its national interests. Thus, the new Africa Policy again prioritizes the wrong area of focus and, along with the 2018 US National Defense Strategy (NDS), articulates a continuing effort to focus on lethality over humanitarian assistance and stabilization and fails to appropriate attention to preventing and ending conflict, while preparing for and stoking the fires of large-scale war with Russia, China, Iran, and North Korea.[43]

The US defense establishment *can* use intelligence solely for targeting when necessary but *should* only use it this way when operationally essential to *directly* feed a singular strategic goal. The machinery that mass-produces targets and approaches to kill them is not the only appropriate use of intelligence analysis. Strategic, long-term, high-level thinking about the conditions that truly threaten US security and economic interests is the purview of strategic intelligence as an unbiased analytic product to inform policymaking. Until policymakers recognize this critical capability as an objective, nonpartisan view of the strategic environment, they will be unable to manage thorny issues like insurgency or the multidomain battle space itself.

While the "War on Terror" has clearly done more harm than good in the places where it has been fought, and on the US and Western reputations around the world, abruptly ending it is not the effective way to consolidate any gains that have come from it. The NDS clearly stated that "Inter-state strategic competition, not terrorism, is now the primary concern in US national security." Until policymakers identify a new grand strategic objective, such as "become fully independent from England," or "Destroy Communism as a viable economic system in the world," and plot its achievement out over the next 50 years, the US will continue to mire itself deeply in the Stabilization Trap with no amount of relational legitimacy able to secure its release.

NOTES

1. *Guiding Principles for Stabilization and Reconstruction,* United States Institute of Peace and U.S. Army Peace Keeping and Stability Operations Institute, 2009, pp. 3–12. Available from https://www.usip.org/sites/default/files/guiding_principles_full.pdf accessed on January 4, 2018.
2. Ambassador Alex Laskaris in a presentation to PKSOI at Carlisle Barracks, Carlisle, PA on August 28, 2017. AMB Laskaris was serving as the Deputy for Civil-Military Engagement to the Commander of US Africa Command at the time. Biography available from https://www.africom.mil/about-the-command/leadership/deputy-to-the-commander-for-civil-military-engagement accessed on February 29, 2019.
3. Dr. Donovan C. Chau, *U.S. Counterterrorism in Sub-Saharan Africa: Understanding Costs, Cultures, and Conflicts,* Carlisle, PA: Strategic Studies Institute, U.S. Army War College, August 27, 2008, p. 6. Available from www.strategicstudiesinstitute.army.mil/pubs/display.cfm?pubID=821 accessed on March 12, 2018.
4. Dr. Jennifer Keister, "The Illusion of Chaos: Why Ungoverned Spaces Aren't Ungoverned and Why that Matters." *Cato Institute Policy Analysis,* No. 766, December 2014. Available from https://www.cato.org/publications/policy-analysis/illusion-chaos-why-ungoverned-spaces-arent-ungoverned-why-matters accessed on March 29, 2018.
5. Arwa Ibrahim, "Muqtada al-Sadr: Iraq's militia leader turned champion of poor," *Al Jazeera.* Available from https://www.aljazeera.com/indepth/features/muqtada-al-sadr-iraq-militia-leader-turned-champion-poor-180517053738881.html accessed on May 17, 2018.
6. "Al-Sadr calls on Iraqis 'to resist'," *Al Jazeera,* January 8, 2011. Available from https://www.aljazeera.com/news/middleeast/2011/01/2011872647305497.html accessed on May 17, 2018.
7. Mustafa al-Kadhimi, "The New Muqtada al-Sadr Seeks Moderate Image," Iraq-Business News, March 13, 2013. Available from http://www.iraq-businessnews.com/2013/03/13/the-new-muqtada-al-sadr-seeks-moderate-image/ accessed on May 17, 2018.
8. Transparency International's Corruption Perception Index (CPI) released on February 21, 2018. Available from https://www.transparency.org/news/feature/corruption_perceptions_index_2017#table accessed on May 17, 2018.
9. Mark Joseph Stern, "How did Hamas Take Control of the Gaza Strip?" Slate, November 19, 2012. Available from http://www.slate.com/articles/news_and_politics/explainer/2012/11/hamas_in_gaza_how_the_organization_beat_fatah_and_took_control_of_the_gaza.html accessed on May 17, 2018.

10. "Profile: Egypt's Muslim Brotherhood," BBC, last updated on December 25, 2013. Available from http://www.bbc.com/news/world-middle-east-12313405 accessed on May 17, 2018.
11. Nadia Schadlow, *The Art of Governance: Consolidating Combat Success into Political Victory*, Washington, DC: Georgetown University Press, 2017, p. 146.
    In Nadia Schadlow, *The Art of Governance: Consolidating Combat Success into Political Victory*, Washington, DC: Georgetown University Press, 2017, p. 146.
12. Oral history interview with Lucius D. Clay, July 16, 1947, conducted by Richard McKinzie, as reported in Nadia Schadlow, *The Art of Governance: Consolidating Combat Success into Political Victory*, Washington, DC: Georgetown University Press, 2017, p. 146.
13. LTC Steve Lewis, "Good Governance and the Counterstate: Consolidating Unconventional Gains," in *2017–2018 Civil Affairs Issue Papers: Civil Affairs: A Force for Consolidating Gains, PKSOI Papers* Volume 4, 2018, p. 68. Available from http://pksoi.armywarcollege.edu/index.cfm/resources/pksoi-publications/ accessed on May 7, 2018.
    Unconventional warfare is defined as "activities conducted to enable a resistance movement or insurgency to coerce, disrupt, or overthrow a government or occupying power by operating through or within an underground, auxiliary, and guerilla force in a denied area." Reference: Joint Publication 3-05, Special operations, July 2014. Available from www.jcs.mil/Portals/36/Documents/Doctrine/pubs/jp3_05.pdf accessed on May 7, 2018.
14. Department of Defense Directive, 2000.13, Washington, DC: Department of Defense Undersecretary of Defense (Policy), March 11, 2014, pp. 1–2. http://www.dtic.mil/whs/directives/corres/pdf/200013_2014_correction_b.pdf accessed December 24, 2016.
15. Department of Defense Directive, 2000.13, Washington, DC: Department of Defense Undersecretary of Defense (Policy), March 11, 2014, p. 3. http://www.dtic.mil/whs/directives/corres/pdf/200013_2014_correction_b.pdf accessed on December 24, 2016.
16. Quote reference is COL Jay Liddick, "Army Operational Effectiveness Requires Changes to Its Civil Affairs Capability," *U.S. Army War College Strategic Research Paper*, January 4, 2017, p. 4. Available from publications.armywarcollege.edu/pubs/3451.pdf accessed on July 27, 2018. COL Liddick's paper provides a useful summary of modern CA history, which does not require replication in this publication.
17. COL Jay Liddick, "Army Operational Effectiveness Requires Changes to Its Civil Affairs Capability," *U.S. Army War College Strategic Research Paper*, January 4, 2017, p. 10. Available from publications.armywarcollege.edu/pubs/3451.pdf accessed on July 27, 2018.

18. United States Army Special Operations History Office, *U.S. Army Civil Affairs History Handbook*, Fort Bragg, North Carolina: USASOC History Office, 2016, p. 22.

19. COL Jay Liddick, "Army Operational Effectiveness Requires Changes to Its Civil Affairs Capability," U.S. Army War College Strategic Research Paper, January 4, 2017, p. 10. Available from publications.armywarcollege.edu/pubs/3451.pdf accessed on July 27, 2018.

20. Majors Arnel P. David and Clay Daniels, "Strategic misfire: The Army's planned reduction of Civil Affairs forces," Foreign Policy "Best Defense series," May 12, 2016. Available from http://foreignpolicy.com/2016/05/12/strategic-misfire-the-armys-planned-reduction-of-civil-affairs-forces/ accessed on May 8, 2018.

21. COL Jay Liddick, "Army Operational Effectiveness Requires Changes to Its Civil Affairs Capability," *U.S. Army War College Strategic Research Paper*, January 4, 2017, p. 20. Available from publications.armywarcollege.edu/pubs/3451.pdf accessed on July 27, 2018.

22. Russell W. Glenn, "Ten Million is Not Enough: Coming to Grips with Megacities' Challenges and Opportunities," *Small Wars Journal*, January 25, 2017. Available from http://smallwarsjournal.com/jrnl/art/ten-million-is-not-enough-coming-to-grips-with-megacities%E2%80%99-challenges-and-opportunities#_ednref18 accessed on March 7, 2018.

23. The paragraph continues, "These methods may include intimidation, sabotage and subversion, propaganda, terror, and military pressure. Sometimes insurgents attempt to organize the populace into a mass movement. At a minimum, they aim to make effective host-nation governance impossible. Some insurgencies are transnational. Other situations involve multiple insurgencies in one area at the same time. Counterinsurgency becomes more complex in these situations. Paramount to successful counterinsurgency operations are stability activities aimed at increasing host-nation government legitimacy by providing services and security to the local populace." *U.S. Army Doctrine Reference Publication on Stability 3-07 (ADRP 3-07)*, August 2012, pp. 3–17–18, Para 3–102. Available from https://armypubs.army.mil/epubs/DR_pubs/DR_a/pdf/web/adrp3_07.pdf accessed on July 27, 2018.

24. *U.S. Army Doctrine Reference Publication on Stability 3-07 (ADRP 3-07)*, August 2012, pp. 3–22, Para 3–122. Available from https://armypubs.army.mil/epubs/DR_pubs/DR_a/pdf/web/adrp3_07.pdf accessed on July 27, 2018.

25. DRAFT *U.S. Army Doctrine Reference Publication on Stability 3-07 (ADRP 3-07)*, pp. 3–12 Para 3–72. The author reviewed this revised version in April 2018; it is still undergoing Army review and has not been made publicly available as of publication of this monograph.

26. David Kilcullen describes this in his *Out of the Mountains: The Coming Age of the Urban Guerrilla*, London, UK: Oxford University Press, 2013, pp. 174–75, defining "pre-conflict sensing—trying to understand as much as possible about a given environment before it gets into crisis, so that we know the relationships among different actors in the society, understand the extent of different groups territorial control or popular support, and can track flows and patterns in cities and towns that explain their systems logic—will be critically important." He further emphasizes that this "need not involve anything intrusive or underhanded—no nefarious sneaking around or spying—since most of what we need to know is open-source information, is already being gathered and published by local people and civil society organizations, or is well known to diasporas in our own countries."

27. While there are many sources where parties express such concerns, one focused on the peace keeping mission environment is "Improving U.N. Situational Awareness: Enhancing the U.N.'s Ability to Prevent and Respond to Mass Human Suffering and to Ensure the Safety and Security of Its Personnel," by Haidi Wilmot of the Stimson Center, published in August 2017, which stated on page 59 "U.N. human rights actors are concerned about sharing information that might expose or compromise sources. U.N. country teams also have some reservations, knowing that displeasing the host government can result in expulsion. It must be made clear to all, therefore, that U.N. staff are in no circumstances being asked to spy or collect information beyond their mandate. Nor are they being asked to share with other U.N. actors, information that might compromise sources or operations. In fact, streams of raw information are often less helpful than information that has been cleaned of sensitive detail, contextualized, and analyzed. What U.N. actors are being asked to do is to contribute curated information and partake in analytical processes." Available from https://www.stimson.org/content/improving-un-situational-awareness accessed on May 2, 2018.

28. Kalume Kazungu and Mohamed Ahmed, "Poor communication, low morale derail battle against Shabaab," *Daily Nation* (Kenya), January 28, 2018. Available from https://www.nation.co.ke/news/war-on-Shabaab-has-dragged-on-inthree-counties-/1056-4282534-8wi48hz/index.html accessed via OE Watch, a foreign news sampler by U.S. Foreign Military Studies Office, Volume 8, Issue #3, March 2018 on March 7, 2018.

29. Kalume Kazungu and Mohamed Ahmed, "Poor communication, low morale derail battle against Shabaab," *Daily Nation* (Kenya), January 28, 2018. Available from https://www.nation.co.ke/news/war-on-Shabaab-has-dragged-on-inthree-counties-/1056-4282534-8wi48hz/index.html accessed via OE Watch, a foreign news sampler by U.S. Foreign Military Studies Office, Volume 8, Issue #3, March 2018 on March 7, 2018.

30. From an editorial in the *Washington Post* that included discussion of Ruchir Sharma's book, Democracy on the Road: A 25-year Journey through India, Fareed Zakaria wrote a column in the *Washington Post* on March 7, 2019 entitled, "The Mueller report will be a test of American democracy. How will we handle it?" Available from https://www.washingtonpost.com/opinions/the-mueller-report-will-be-a-test-of-american-democracy-how-will-we-handle-it/2019/03/07/dc85689c-4121-11e9-922c-64d6b7840b82_story.html?utm_term=.36264d3012f3, accessed on March 14, 2019.

31. Caroline Houck, "'We're Finding It Difficult to Hold' Territory in Somalia: [U.S.] Senator," *Defense One* March 2, 2018. Available from http://www.defenseone.com/threats/2018/03/were-finding-it-difficult-hold-territory-somalia-senator/146376/?oref=defenseone_today_nl accessed on March 2, 2018.

32. "Special Inspector General for Afghanistan Reconstruction Report SIGAR-14-49-SP Fact Sheet: CERP Priorities and Spending in Afghanistan FY 2004-2014," U.S. Central Command Joint Logistics (J4) Directorate Comments, p. 17. Available from https://www.sigar.mil/pdf/special%20projects/SIGAR-15-49-SP.pdf accessed on March 29, 2018.

33. "Follow-Up on a Department of Defense Audit of Commander's Emergency Response Program Funds Provided to USAID/Afghanistan," Report No. F-306-14-003-S, September 7, 2014. Available from pdf. usaid.gov/pdf_docs/PDACY487.pdf accessed on March 29, 2018.

34. Gregory Johnson, Vijaya Ramachandran, and Julie Walz, "CERP in Afghanistan: Refining Military Capabilities in Development Activities," *Prism*, Vol. 3, No. 2, p. 84, January 2012. Available from cco.ndu.edu/Portals/96/Documents/prism/prism_3-2/prism81-98_johnson-all.pdf accessed on March 29, 2018.

35. Daniel Egel, Charles P. Ries, et al. "Investing in the Fight: Assessing the Use of the Commander's Emergency Response Program in Afghanistan," *Rand Report*, 2016. Available from www.rand.org/pubs/research_reports/RR1508.html accessed on March 29, 2018.

36. Gregory Johnson, Vijaya Ramachandran, and Julie Walz, "CERP in Afghanistan: Refining Military Capabilities in Development Activities," *Prism*, Vol. 3, No. 2, p. 96. Available from http://cco.ndu.edu/Portals/96/Documents/prism/prism_3-2/prism81-98_johnson-all.pdf accessed on March 29, 2018.

37. Rebecca Patterson, "Revisiting a School of Military Government: How Reanimating a World War II-Era Institution Could Professionalize Military Nation Building," Ewing Marion Kauffman Foundation, June 2011, p. 18. Available from https://papers.ssrn.com/sol3/papers.cfm?abstract_id=1879444 accessed on May 7, 2018.

38. Nadia Schadlow, *War and the Art of Governance: Consolidating Combat Success into Political Victory*, Washington, DC: Georgetown University Press, p. 262.
39. John Bolton, "Remarks by National Security Advisor Ambassador John R. Bolton on the Trump Administration's New Africa Strategy," December 13, 2018, Heritage Foundation, Washington, D.C. Available from https://www.whitehouse.gov/briefings-statements/remarks-national-security-advisor-ambassador-john-r-bolton-trump-administrations-new-africa-strategy/ accessed on February 29, 2019.
40. May Ying Welsh, "Making sense of Mali's armed groups," *Al Jazeera*, January 17, 2013. Available from https://www.aljazeera.com/indepth/features/2013/01/20131139522812326.html accessed on March 22, 2018.
41. "Oct 2017 Niger Ambush Summary of Investigation," U.S. Department of Defense unclassified summary report released on May 10, 2018. Available from https://dod.defense.gov/portals/1/features/2018/0418_niger/img/Oct-2017-Niger-Ambush-Summary-of-Investigation.pdf accessed on March 11, 2019.
42. Daniella Diaz, "Key senators say they didn't know the US had troops in Niger," Cable News Network (CNN) news report, October 23, 2017. Available from https://www.cnn.com/2017/10/23/politics/niger-troops-lawmakers/index.html accessed on March 11, 2019.
43. "National Defense Strategy of the United States of America, 2018" U.S. Department of Defense, February 2018. Available from https://dod.defense.gov/Portals/1/Documents/pubs/2018-National-Defense-Strategy-Summary.pdf accessed on March 11, 2019.

Index[1]

[1] Note: Page numbers followed by 'n' refer to notes.

© The Author(s) 2020   71
D. E. Chido, *Strategic Intelligence and Civil Affairs
to Understand Legitimacy and Insurgency*,
https://doi.org/10.1007/978-3-030-20977-3

Printed by Printforce, the Netherlands